GCSE OCR 21st Century Additional Science Foundation Workbook

This book is for anyone doing **GCSE OCR 21st Century Additional Science** at foundation level.

It's full of **tricky questions**... each one designed to make you **sweat** — because that's the only way you'll get any **better**.

There are questions to see **what facts** you know. There are questions to see how well you can **apply those facts**. And there are questions to see what you know about **how science works**.

It's also got some daft bits in to try and make the whole experience at least vaguely entertaining for you.

What CGP is all about

Our sole aim here at CGP is to produce the highest quality books — carefully written, immaculately presented and dangerously close to being funny.

Then we work our socks off to get them out to you — at the cheapest possible prices.

Contents

Module B4 — Homeostasis
The Basics of Homeostasis 1
Diffusion and Osmosis 2
Enzymes 4
Controlling Body Temperature 5
Controlling Water Content 7
Treating Kidney Failure 9

Module C4 — Chemical Patterns
Atoms 11
Atoms in Chemical Reactions 12
Line Spectrums 13
The Periodic Table 14
Electron Shells 16
Group 1 — The Alkali Metals 17
Group 7 — Halogens 18
Laboratory Safety 20
Ionic Bonding 21

Module P4 — Explaining Motion
Speed 22
Speed and Velocity 23
Velocity 25
Forces and Friction 26
Forces and Motion 27
Work 30
Kinetic Energy 31
Gravitational Potential Energy 32
Bungee Jumping 34

Module B5 — Growth and Development
DNA — Making Proteins 36
Cell Division — Mitosis 37
Cell Division — Meiosis 38
Development from a Single Cell 39
Growth in Plants 40
Stem Cells and Parkinson's 42

Module C5 — Chemicals of the Natural Environment
Chemicals in the Atmosphere 43
Chemicals in the Hydrosphere 44
Chemicals in the Lithosphere 45
Chemicals in the Biosphere 47
Metals from Minerals 48
Electrolysis 49
Metals 51
Environmental Impact 52

Module P5 — Electric Circuits

Static Electricity 55
Electric Current 56
Circuits — The Basics 58
Resistance 59
Series Circuits 61
Parallel Circuits 62
Mains Electricity 63
Electrical Energy 66
The National Grid 68

Module B6 — Brain and Mind

The Nervous System 70
Reflexes 73
Brain Development and Learning 75
Studying the Brain 77
Memory Mapping 78

Module C6 — Chemical Synthesis

Industrial Chemical Synthesis 80
Acids and Alkalis 81
Acids Reacting with Metals 83
Oxides, Hydroxides and Carbonates 84
Synthesising Compounds 86
Relative Formula Mass 89
Isolating the Product and Measuring Yield 90
Titrations 91
Purity 92
Rates of Reaction 93
Measuring Rates of Reaction 95

Module P6 — The Wave Model of Radiation

Waves — The Basics 96
Wave Properties 97
Wave Interference 100
Electromagnetic Radiation 102
Uses of EM Waves 103
Adding Information to Waves 105
Analogue and Digital Signals 106
Broadband and Wireless Internet 107

Published by Coordination Group Publications Ltd.

Editors:
Amy Boutal, Ellen Bowness, Tim Burne, Tom Cain, Katherine Craig, Tom Harte, Sarah Hilton, Kate Houghton, Sharon Keeley, Andy Park, Rose Parkin, Ami Snelling, Laurence Stamford, Jane Towle, Julie Wakeling, Sarah Williams.

Contributors:
Michael Aicken, Steve Coggins, Mike Dagless, Jane Davies, Mark A Edwards, Max Fishel, Dr Giles R Greenway, Dr Iona MJ Hamilton, Derek Harvey, Rebecca Harvey, Frederick Langridge, Barbara Mascetti, John Myers, Richard Parsons, Andy Rankin, Adrian Schmit, Sidney Stringer Community School, Claire Stebbing, Pat Szczesniak, Paul Warren, Chris Workman, Dee Wyatt.

ISBN: 978 1 84762 004 0

With thanks to Glenn Rogers for the proofreading.

With thanks to Laura Phillips for the copyright research.

With thanks to Waste Watch, www.wastewatch.org.uk, an environmental organisation working to change how we use the world's natural resources, for the information on page 53.

With thanks to The National Trust for the information on page 68.

Data used to construct pie chart on page 80 from "Concise Dictionary of Chemistry" edited by Daintith, J (1986). By permission of Oxford University Press. www.oup.com

Groovy website: www.cgpbooks.co.uk

Printed by Elanders Hindson Ltd, Newcastle upon Tyne.
Jolly bits of clipart from CorelDRAW®

Text, design, layout and original illustrations © Coordination Group Publications Ltd. 2007
All rights reserved.

Module B4 — Homeostasis

The Basics of Homeostasis

Q1 Homeostasis is an important process in the human body.

a) Use the words in the box to complete the passage about homeostasis.
Some words may be used more than once.

function	changing	constant
The conditions inside the body must be kept .... even when the environment outside is .... — the body cells need the right conditions to .... properly. Homeostasis helps to maintain a .... internal environment.		

b) Give **two** examples of conditions in the body that are controlled by homeostasis.

1. ....

2. ....

Q2 Exercise and climate can both have effects on the body.

a) Circle the correct words in the table to show the effects that **exercise** has on conditions in the body.

Temperature	increases / decreases
Water content	increases / decreases

b) What is the main risk to the body in a very **cold** climate?

....

Q3 The **body control system** has three main parts.
Draw lines to match the parts with what they do.

receptors — receive information and coordinate a response

processing centres — detect stimuli

effectors — produce a response

Top Tips: Some animals don't have such a fancy homeostatic system to control temperature. Some reptiles have to bask in sunlight until their blood has warmed up before they can go about their business. I wouldn't mind lounging around in the sun for a couple of hours before work every day...

Diffusion and Osmosis

Q1 Complete the passage below by circling the correct word in each pair.

> Diffusion is the direct / **random** movement of particles from an area where they are at a **higher** / lower concentration to an area where they are at a higher / **lower** concentration. The rate of diffusion is faster when the difference in concentration is **bigger** / smaller.

Q2 The diagram below shows some **body cells**. A **blood vessel** lies close to the cells.

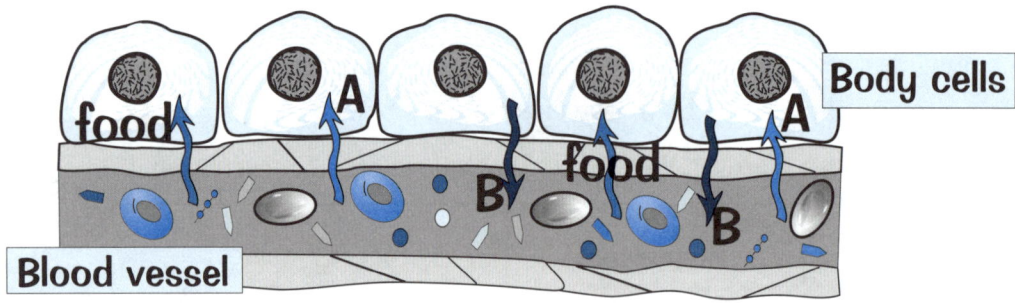

a) Is the concentration of food higher in the **blood** or inside the **cells**?

....

b) Draw a circle around the gas that is represented by:

   i) The arrows labelled A.   **oxygen** / carbon dioxide

   ii) The arrows labelled B.   oxygen / **carbon dioxide**

Q3 Tick the boxes to show whether the following statements are **true** or **false**.

		True	False
a)	Diffusion happens in gases, liquids and solids.	☐	☐
b)	Food moves from the body cells to the blood by diffusion.	☐	☐
c)	Diffusion can't happen across cell membranes.	☐	☐
d)	Oxygen diffuses from the blood into the body cells.	☐	☐

diffusion is an essential life process

Module B4 — Homeostasis

Diffusion and Osmosis

Q4 Fill in the missing words to complete the paragraph.

membrane	sugar	diffusion	dilute
partially	water	concentrated	

Osmosis is the overall movement of .... molecules across a .... permeable .... The molecules move from a more .... to a more .... solution. Osmosis is a special type of ....

Q5 Look at the diagram and answer the questions below.

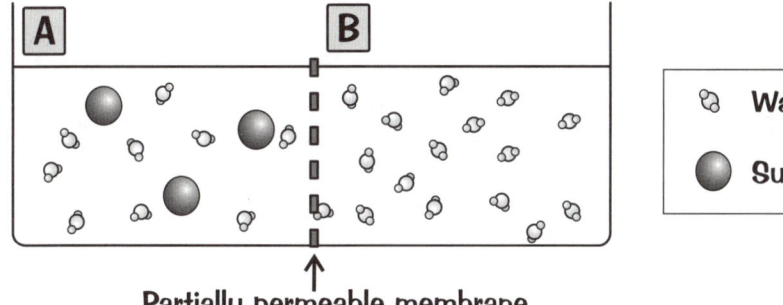

Partially permeable membrane

a) On which side of the membrane is there the **highest** concentration of water molecules? ....

b) Circle the correct words from each pair to describe what will happen.

The liquid level on side B will **rise / fall**, because there is a net flow of water molecules from side **A / B** to side **A / B**.

c) Tick the box next to the correct description of a **partially permeable membrane**.

☐ A membrane that doesn't allow any substances to diffuse through it.

☐ A membrane that only allows certain substances to diffuse through it.

☐ A membrane that allows any substance to diffuse through it.

Top Tips: Osmosis and diffusion are two of the ways that things can move in and out of your cells. Osmosis is just a special type of diffusion involving water molecules. They both happen due to differences in the concentration of particles between regions.

Module B4 — Homeostasis

Enzymes

Q1 a) Circle any of the following statements that correctly describe enzymes.

b) In the box below, draw a sketch to show the 'lock and key' model of enzyme action.

Q2 This graph shows the results from an investigation into the effect of **temperature** on the rate of an **enzyme**-catalysed reaction.

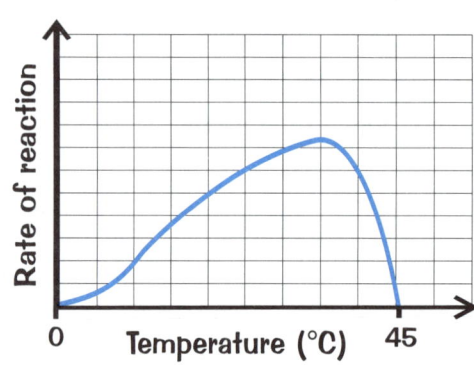

a) What is the **optimum** temperature for this enzyme?

....

b) Use the words in the box to complete the passage.

energy	increases	frequency	decreases

At low temperatures, small increases in temperature increase the .... and .... of collisions between the enzymes and other molecules. This .... the rate of reaction.

c) What happens to the enzymes at 45 °C?

....

Module B4 — Homeostasis

Controlling Body Temperature

Q1 The human body is maintained at a temperature of about **37 °C**.

a) What two things must be balanced to maintain a constant body temperature.

....

b) Name the location in the body of temperature receptors that monitor the:

i) external temperature ....

ii) temperature of the blood ....

c) Use the words in the box to complete the passage to explain how the nervous system controls body temperature.

effectors	blood	muscles	brain	sweat glands

Temperature receptors detect the internal and external temperature and they send this information to the ...., which acts as a processing centre. If the receptors detect that the body temperature is too high or too low, it automatically triggers .... e.g. .... or ....

Q2 The body has a number of **mechanisms** to help control its temperature.

a) i) What process can help the body to **cool down** when it's too hot?

....

ii) Why can this process be dangerous in very hot temperatures?

....

b) Shivering can help the body to **warm up** when it's too cold.

i) Which parts of the body are the **effectors** in shivering?

....

ii) Circle the correct words to describe how shivering helps to increase body temperature.

> The muscles **rapidly** / **slowly** contract, **increasing** / **decreasing** the rate of respiration. Some of the energy released in respiration is given out as heat, which warms the **bone** / **tissue** surrounding the muscles.

Module B4 — Homeostasis

Controlling Body Temperature

Q3 A holiday-maker with severe **heat stroke** is admitted to a hospital in Mexico.

a) List two possible **causes** of the patient's heat stroke.

1. ....

2. ....

In Mexico, really hot chilli can be a cause of heat stroke.

b) Circle the symptoms below that you might expect the patient to exhibit.

dizziness   headaches   diarrhoea   confusion   gain in appetite   increased urine output

c) What happens to the normal mechanisms for controlling body temperature when you get too hot?

....

d) Describe how you would expect the patient to be treated when they first arrive at the hospital.

....

....

....

Q4 A group of **walkers** are found by a mountain rescue team after being missing in **poor weather** conditions on Mount Snowdon for **14 hours**. The mountain rescue team begin to assess the condition of the walkers. One of the walkers has a core body temperature of 34 °C.

a) Draw a circle around the condition that the walker is suffering from.

     dehydration   hypothermia   heat stroke

b) Describe four symptoms the walker might exhibit.

....

....

c) Tick the correct boxes to show which of these treatments the walker should be given.

- ☐ Warm, dry clothing
- ☐ Placed into a bath of very hot water
- ☐ Warmed by a gentle heat source
- ☐ Exposed to very high temperatures, e.g. sitting in front of a roaring fire
- ☐ Have their hands and feet vigorously rubbed to warm up the extremities

Module B4 — Homeostasis

Controlling Water Content

Q1 The body needs to balance its water **input** and **output**.

a) Name three ways that water is **gained** by the body.

1. .... 2. .... 3. ....

b) Name three ways that water is **lost** by the body.

1. .... 2. .... 3. ....

c) Why is it important to maintain a balanced water level?

....

....

Q2 My brother was getting on my nerves, so I put him on a treadmill and turned the setting to high (just to keep him quiet for a bit).

Circle the correct word from each pair to complete the following sentences.

a) He will lose **more / less** water from the skin, because the exercise will **increase / decrease** his temperature — he will have to sweat **more / less** to cool down.

b) He will lose **more / less** water from his lungs, because the exercise will make him breathe harder and **slower / faster** — **more / less** water vapour will be lost via the lungs.

c) He will lose **more / less** water as sweat and in the breath, so to help balance this his kidneys will give out **more / less** water in the urine.

Q3 Use the words in the box to complete the passage below. Some words may be used more than once.

| salt | water | kidney | sugar |
| protein | urea | bladder | blood cells |

Kidneys filter substances out of the blood, including ....,

............................, ... and ....

All the .... is reabsorbed and as much ....

and .... as the body needs.

The remaining urine is stored in the ....

Module B4 — Homeostasis

Controlling Water Content

Q4 The **concentration** of urine and **amount** of urine produced are affected by many factors.

a) List three things that affect the **amount** and **concentration** of urine.

1. ....
2. ....
3. ....

b) Tick the boxes to show whether the following statements are **true** or **false**.

	True	False
i) When you drink too little you will produce concentrated urine.	☐	☐
ii) On a hot day you will produce less concentrated urine than on a cold day.	☐	☐
iii) Drinking a lot of water will produce a large amount of urine.	☐	☐
iv) Drinking a lot of water will produce dilute urine.	☐	☐
v) Exercising will produce less concentrated urine than resting will.	☐	☐

Q5 **Drugs** can affect the water content of the body.

a) Circle the correct word from each pair to complete the passage about the effect of **alcohol** on the water content of the body.

> Alcohol causes the kidneys to reabsorb **more** / **less** water than they usually do.
> This results in a **smaller** / **larger** amount of more **dilute** / **concentrated** urine
> being produced, which can lead to **dehydration** / **overhydration**.

b) i) Name another drug that can interfere with the body's water level.

....

ii) How does this drug affect the amount and concentration of urine produced?

....

Top Tips: Kidneys do loads of important jobs and that's why kidney failure is so dangerous. You can live with only one kidney and so it is possible for some people with kidney failure to receive a donated kidney from a member of their family or from another suitable donor (see next page).

Module B4 — Homeostasis

Treating Kidney Failure

Q1   Read the passage below and then answer the questions that follow.

Treating Kidney Failure

Around 40 000 people in the UK suffer from serious kidney failure. When the kidneys aren't working properly, waste substances build up in the blood. Without treatment, kidney failure is eventually fatal.

Two key treatments are currently available for patients with kidney failure: dialysis — where machines do some of the jobs of the kidneys, or a kidney transplant.

Dialysis

Dialysis has to be performed regularly to keep the concentrations of dissolved substances in the blood at normal levels, and to remove waste substances.

In a dialysis machine the person's blood flows alongside a partially permeable barrier, surrounded by a special dialysis fluid. The membrane is permeable to things like dissolved salts and waste substances, but not to big molecules like proteins — this mimics the membranes in a healthy kidney. The dialysis fluid has the same concentration of dissolved salt and glucose as healthy blood. This means that useful dissolved salt and glucose won't be lost from the blood during dialysis. Only waste substances (such as urea), excess salt and water diffuse across the barrier.

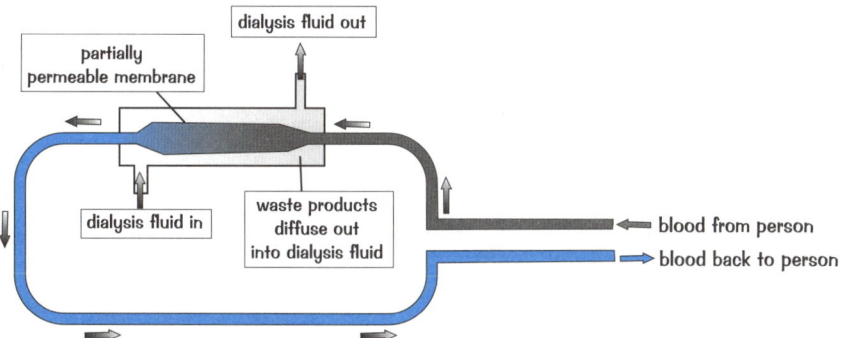

Patients with kidney failure generally need to have a dialysis session three times a week. Dialysis can be a very time-consuming process — each session can take over 3 hours.

Transplantation

Some patients are offered a kidney transplant. Healthy kidneys are usually transplanted from people who have died suddenly, and who are on the organ donor register or carry a donor card (provided their relatives give the go-ahead). A kidney can also be transplanted from live donors — as we all have two of them and can live with just one.

Kidney transplantation has a high success rate but sometimes the donor kidney is rejected by the patient's immune system. The risk of rejection is minimised in the following ways:

- A donor with a tissue type that closely matches the patient is chosen.
- The patient's bone marrow is zapped with radiation to stop white blood cells being produced — so they won't attack the transplanted kidney. They also have to take drugs that suppress the immune system.

Module B4 — Homeostasis

Treating Kidney Failure

a) A model of **dialysis** is shown below. No movement of substances has taken place yet.

   i) Which two particles will **not** diffuse across the membrane from the bloodstream into the dialysis fluid?

   1. ....

   2. ....

   ii) Suggest why these particles won't diffuse across the membrane.

   ....

   iii) Which substance's concentration will increase in the dialysis fluid?

   ....

   iv) What do you notice about the concentration of glucose on either side of the membrane? Suggest a reason for this.

   ....

   ....

b) The steps in dialysis are listed below. Number the steps in the correct order by writing 1 to 5 in the boxes. The first one has been done for you.

   ☐ Excess water, ions and wastes are filtered out of the blood and pass into the dialysis fluid.

   ☐ The patient's blood flows into the dialysis machine and between partially permeable membranes.

   ☐ Blood is returned to the patient's body via a vein in their arm.

   ☐ Dialysis continues until nearly all the waste and excess substances are removed.

   [1] A needle is inserted into a blood vessel in the patient's arm to remove blood.

c) i) Give an advantage that a transplant has over dialysis for a patient with kidney failure.

   ....

   ii) Give two precautions used to try and prevent a patient's body from rejecting a new kidney.

   1. ....

   2. ....

Module B4 — Homeostasis

Module C4 — Chemical Patterns

Atoms

Q1 Draw lines to match each part of an atom with the correct description.

- neutron
- nucleus
- electron

- It moves around the nucleus in shells.
- It's heavy and has no charge.
- It's in the centre of the atom and contains protons and neutrons.

Q2 Draw a diagram of a **helium atom** in the space provided and label each type of **particle** on your diagram.

Helium has 2 of each type of particle.

Q3 **Complete** this table.

Particle	Mass	Charge
Proton	1	
		0
Electron	0.0005	

Top Tips: Learn all this stuff about atoms and you've already got a good bit of basic chemistry. Make sure you know the different parts of an atom — protons, neutrons, electrons, the nucleus and those funky shells floating around the edge. They all fit together perfectly to form an atom — the building blocks of everything.

Atoms in Chemical Reactions

Q1 Circle the correct words to complete the following sentences.

a) Neutral atoms have a charge of **0** / **–1**.

b) A charged particle is called an **element** / **ion**.

c) A neutral atom has **the same** / **a different** number of protons and electrons.

d) If an electron is added to a neutral atom, the atom becomes **negatively** / **positively** charged.

e) The number of **protons** / **neutrons** in an atom tells you what element it is.

Q2 Complete the table below to show the number of **protons** and **electrons** in an atom of each element.

element	electrons	protons
magnesium	12	
carbon		6
oxygen		

Use a periodic table to help you with this question.

Q3 **Sodium** (Na) reacts with **water** (H_2O) to produce **sodium hydroxide** (NaOH) and **hydrogen** (H_2).

a) What state symbol would be used in the equation for the above reaction:

   i) water? ....

   ii) hydrogen gas? ....

b) What are the **reactants** and the **products** in this reaction?

   Reactants: ....

   Products: ....

c) Write the **word equation** for this reaction.

   ....

Line Spectrums

Q1 A scientist is carrying out a **flame test** to identify the **metals** present in three different compounds.

  a) Complete the following sentence about flame tests.

  > Some elements give a distinctive ....
  > when placed in a ....

  b) Draw lines to match the flame colours the scientist sees to the metal that is present.

  yellow/orange   lithium

  red   sodium

  lilac   potassium

Q2 a) Use the words in the box to complete the passage about **line spectrums**. Some words may be used more than once.

> light   element   line
> elements   excited   electron   electrons
>
> When heated, the .... in an atom become
> .... and release energy as ....
> The wavelengths of .... emitted can be recorded as a
> .... spectrum. Different .... emit
> different wavelengths of .... due to their different
> .... arrangements. This means that each
> .... will produce a different ....
> spectrum, allowing them to be identified.

  b) As well as to help identify elements, what else have line spectrums been used for?

  ....

Top Tips: I don't know why atoms get so excited when they're stuck in a hot flame — it certainly doesn't appeal to me. There's no accounting for some tastes... Anyway, line spectrums aren't as tricky as they might seem at first. Stick at it — they could easily come up in the exam — and you'll be passing with, errr... flying colours...

Module C4 — Chemical Patterns

The Periodic Table

Q1 Use a **periodic table** to help you answer the following questions.

a) Name one element in the same period as silicon. ....

b) Name one element in the same group as potassium. ....

c) Name one element that is a halogen. ....

d) Name one element that is an alkali metal. ....

Q2 **Complete** this table.

Name	Symbol	Relative atomic mass	Proton number
Iron	Fe	56	
	Pb	207	
Xenon			54
Copper			

Q3 Choose from the words below to fill in the blanks in each sentence.

| left-hand | right-hand | horizontal | similar | different |
| vertical | metals | non-metals | increasing | decreasing |

a) A group in the periodic table is a .... line of elements.

b) Most of the elements in the periodic table are ....

c) Elements in the periodic table are arranged in order of .... proton number.

d) Non-metals are on the .... side of the periodic table.

e) Elements in the same group have .... properties.

Top Tips: The periodic table does more than just tell you the names and symbols of all the elements. You can get some other pretty important information from it too. For starters, it's all arranged in a useful pattern which means that elements with similar properties form columns.

Module C4 — Chemical Patterns

The Periodic Table

Q4 Tick the correct boxes to show whether these statements are **true** or **false**.

                                                                                                      True False

a) The rows in the periodic table are also known as periods.

b) Each column in the periodic table contains elements with similar properties.

c) The periodic table is made up of all the known compounds.

d) There are more than 70 known elements.

e) Each new period in the periodic table represents another full shell of electrons.

Q5 Argon is an extremely **unreactive** gas. Use the periodic table to give the names of two more gases that you would expect to have similar properties to argon.

1. ....

2. ....

Q6 Elements in the same group undergo **similar reactions**.

a) Tick the pairs of elements that would undergo similar reactions.

        A potassium and rubidium

        B helium and fluorine

        C calcium and oxygen

        D nitrogen and arsenic

b) How does the periodic table show that fluorine and chlorine would undergo similar reactions? Circle the correct answer.

    Fluorine and chlorine are in the same group.

    Fluorine and chlorine are in the same period (horizontal row).

    Fluorine and chlorine are the same element.

Module C4 — Chemical Patterns

Electron Shells

Q1 Tick the boxes to show whether each statement is **true** or **false**.

                                                                                                True False

   a) Electrons occupy shells in atoms.

   b) The highest energy levels are always filled first.

   c) Elements in Group 0 have a full outer shell of electrons.

   d) Reactive elements have full outer shells.

Q2 What is **wrong** with this diagram? Circle the correct statements.

The outer shell doesn't contain enough electrons.

There should be two electrons in the inner shell.

The outer shell contains too many electrons.

There should be eight electrons in the inner shell.

Use a periodic table to help you with this question.

Q3 Write out the **electron configurations** for the following elements.

   a) Beryllium ....   **d)** Calcium ....

   b) Oxygen ....   **e)** Aluminium ....

   c) Silicon ....   **f)** Argon ....

Q4 **Chlorine** has an atomic number of 17.

   a) What is its electron configuration? ....

   b) Draw the electrons on the shells in the diagram.

Module C4 — Chemical Patterns

Group 1 — Alkali Metals

Q1 Sodium, potassium and lithium are all alkali metals.

a) Highlight the location of the alkali metals on this periodic table.

b) Put sodium, potassium and lithium in order of increasing reactivity and state their symbols.

least reactive ....

....

most reactive ....

c) Complete the sentence below to describe the appearance of the alkali metals.

Alkali metals are .... and have a silvery colour when freshly cut, but .... quickly in moist air.

Q2 Circle the correct words to complete the passage below.

> Sodium is a soft metal with **one** / **two** electron(s) in its outer shell. It reacts vigorously with water, producing **sodium dioxide** / **sodium hydroxide** and **hydrogen** / **oxygen** gas.

Q3 Archibald put a piece of lithium into a beaker of water.

a) Why does the lithium float on top of the water? Circle the correct answer.

Lithium is more dense than water.   **Lithium is less dense than water.**

Lithium has the same density as water.

b) What solution is made by this reaction? Is it acidic, neutral or alkaline?

....

c) i) Write a **word equation** for the reaction between sodium and water.

....

ii) Would you expect the reaction between sodium and water to be **more** or **less** vigorous than the reaction between lithium and water? Explain your answer.

....

Module C4 — Chemical Patterns

Group 7 — Halogens

Q1 Highlight the location of the halogens on this periodic table.

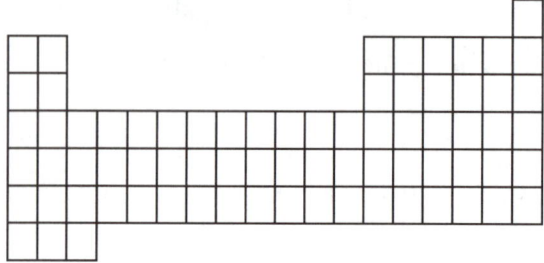

Q2 Draw lines to match each halogen to its correct **symbol**, **description** and relative **reactivity**.

HALOGEN	SYMBOL	DESCRIPTION	REACTIVITY
fluorine	Cl	grey solid	most reactive
chlorine	I	red-brown liquid	least reactive
bromine	Br	yellow gas	quite reactive
iodine	F	green gas	very reactive

Q3 Tick the boxes to show whether the statements below are **true** or **false**.   True   False

a) Chlorine gas is made up of molecules which each contain three chlorine atoms.   ☐ ☐

b) The halogens can kill bacteria in water.   ☐ ☐

c) The halogens become darker in colour as you move down the group.   ☐ ☐

d) All the halogens have seven outer electrons.   ☐ ☐

Q4 Add the phrases to the table to show how the properties of the halogens change as you go **down** the group.

the melting points of the halogens   *the reactivity of the halogens*
the boiling points of the halogens

Increases down the group	Decreases down the group

Module C4 — Chemical Patterns

Group 7 — Halogens

Q5 Sodium was reacted with bromine vapour using the equipment shown. White crystals of a new solid were formed during the reaction.

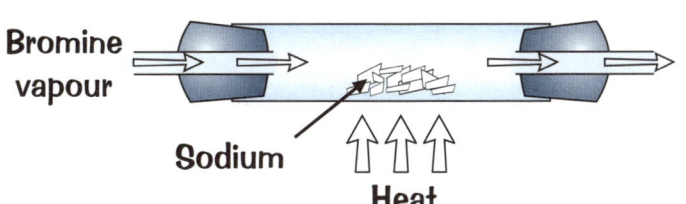

a) Name the white crystals.

....

b) Would you expect the above reaction to be **faster** or **slower** than a similar reaction between:

i) sodium and **iodine** vapour? Explain your answer.

....

ii) sodium and **chlorine** vapour? Explain your answer.

....

Q6 Equal volumes of **bromine water** were added to two test tubes, each containing a different **potassium halide solution**. The results are shown in the table.

SOLUTION	RESULT
potassium chloride	no colour change
potassium iodide	colour change

a) Why was there no colour change when bromine water was added to potassium chloride solution?

....
....

b) Write a **word equation** for the reaction in the potassium iodide solution.

....

c) Would you expect a reaction between bromine water and potassium fluoride? Explain your answer.

Think about where these halogens are in the periodic table.

....
....

Module C4 — Chemical Patterns

Laboratory Safety

Q1 Fill in the meaning of each hazard symbol by choosing the correct label from the box.

> corrosive   toxic   irritant
> harmful   highly flammable   oxidising

a) ....

b) ....

c) ....

d) ....

e) ....

f) ....

Q2 Tick the correct boxes to show whether the following statements are **true** or **false**.

                                                                                                        True   False

a) Alkali metals should be stored under oil.

b) Apparatus that is going to come into contact with an alkali metal should be wet.

c) Safety glasses should be worn whilst using alkali metals.

d) It's safe to touch alkali metals with bare hands.

Q3 The **halogens** must be dealt with very carefully.

a) Why must the halogens only be used inside a fume cupboard?

....

....

b) Liquid bromine is **corrosive**. Explain what this means.

....

Top Tips: Laboratory safety isn't something that you can afford to skim over. It's important both for your exam and for when you're working in the lab. Unfortunately it's not enough to know that a symbol means that a chemical is dangerous — you need to know how it's dangerous.

Module C4 — Chemical Patterns

Ionic Bonding

Q1 Fill in the gaps in the sentences below by choosing the correct words from the box.

> protons   charged particles   repelled by
> electrons   ions   attracted to   neutral particles

a) In ionic bonding atoms lose or gain .... to form ....

b) Ions are ....

c) Ions with opposite charges are strongly .... each other.

Q2 Use this **diagram** to answer the following questions.

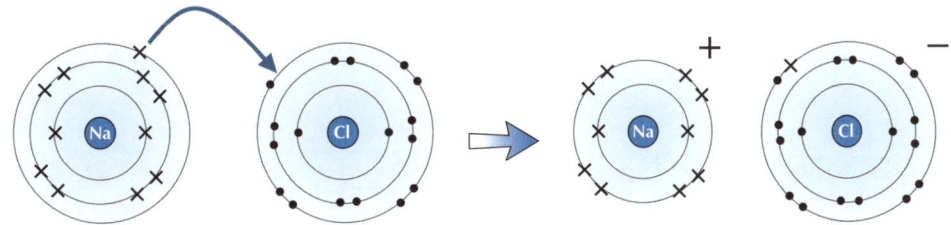

a) How many electrons does **chlorine** need to gain to get a full outer shell of electrons? ....

b) What sort of charge does a **sodium ion** have? ....

c) What is the chemical formula of **sodium chloride**? ....

Q3 Tick the correct boxes to show whether the following statements are **true** or **false**.   True False

a) Metals generally have fewer electrons in their outer shells than non-metals.   ☐ ☐

b) Metals tend to form negatively charged ions.   ☐ ☐

c) Elements in Group 7 gain electrons when they react.   ☐ ☐

d) Atoms form ions in order to get a full outer shell.   ☐ ☐

e) Elements in Group 0 are very reactive.   ☐ ☐

Top Tips: Ionic bonding can be a bit confusing with all that chopping and changing of electrons. Just work through it slowly, making sure you know what groups are likely to lose or gain electrons and whether they'll form positive or negative ions.

Module C4 — Chemical Patterns

Speed

Q1 Indicate whether the following statements are **true** or **false**.

                                                                                                         True False

    a) The speedometer in a car shows its instantaneous speed.

    b) Instantaneous speed is the average speed of an object over a long period of time.

    c) Speed can be measured in metres per second.

Q2 Gemma is racing snails and wants to work out each snail's **speed**.

    a) Gemma draws a distance-time graph for each snail. Which snail was the quickest? Circle the correct answer.

            Snail 1   Snail 2   Snail 3

    b) Gemma finds that the winning snail travelled **0.5 m** in **40 seconds**. Calculate the snail's average speed.

        ....

Q3 I rode my bike **1500 m** to the shops. It took me **5 minutes**.

    a) Calculate how many seconds there are in 5 minutes.

        ....

    b) What was my speed in m/s?

        ....

    c) What type of speed have you just calculated? Circle the correct answer.   **instantaneous / average**

Q4 The diagram below shows a car passing in front of a **speed camera**. The two pictures show the position of the car **0.2 s** apart. The distance between each white line on the road is **2 m**.

    The section of road in the diagram has a **speed limit** of **22 m/s** (50 mph).

    a) How far does the car travel in the time between the two pictures? ....

    b) Find the car's speed.

        ....

    c) Did the car break the speed limit? ....

Speed and Velocity

Q1 Indicate whether the following statements are **true** or **false**.

a) Speed can be positive or negative.

b) Velocity is a speed with a direction.

c) Velocity is a vector.

d) The steeper the gradient of a distance-time graph, the lower the speed.

Q2 Bruce and Clint are having a water pistol shoot-out. They both start from point A and walk 3 m in opposite directions before turning and squirting.

If Clint is **+3 m** away from point A, at what position is Bruce relative to point A? Circle the correct answer.

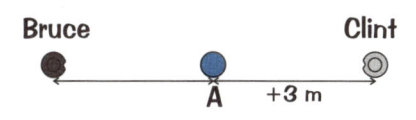

+3 m   0 m   −3 m   −6 m

Q3 A **hare** challenges a **tortoise** to a **race**. The hare is so confident he'll win that he takes a nap on the way — but he sleeps too long and the tortoise ends up winning. Here are some facts and figures about the race:

The **tortoise** ran at a constant speed of **5 m/s** throughout the race — pretty impressive.

The **hare** ran **3000 m** in **300 s** before falling asleep. He slept for **600 s** and then carried on at the **same velocity** as before towards the finish line.

The length of the **race track** was **5000 m**.

a) What was the hare's velocity before he fell asleep? Circle the correct answer.

10 m/s   0.01 m/s   100 m/s   1 m/s

b) Add the information about the hare's run to the graph below.

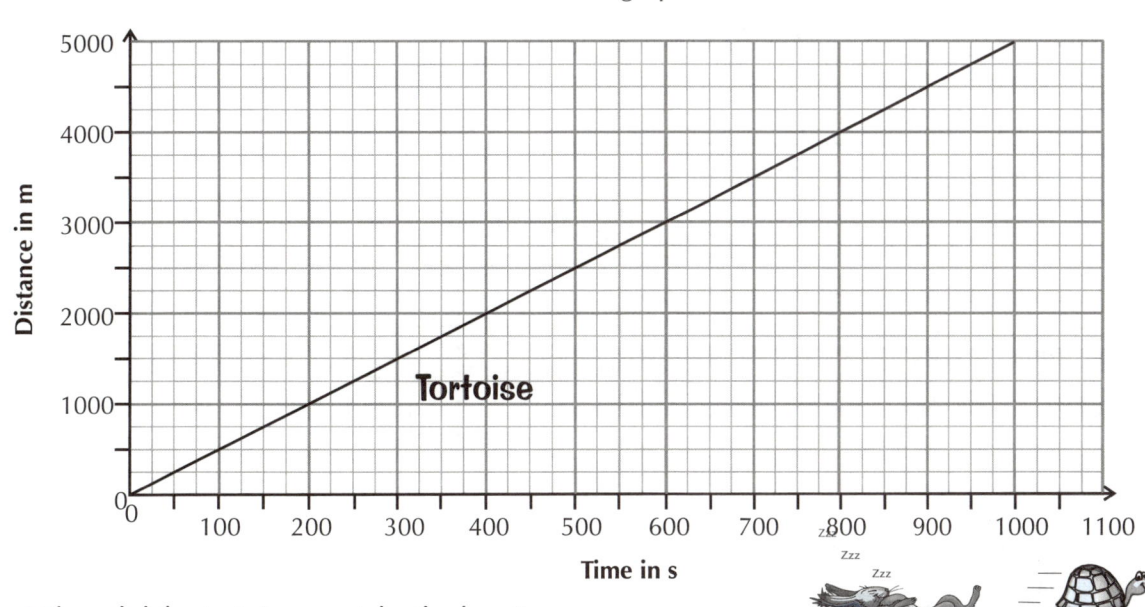

c) When did the tortoise overtake the hare?

....

Module P4 — Explaining Motion

Speed and Velocity

Q4 Steve walked to football training only to find that he'd left his boots at home. He turned round and walked back home, where he spent **30 seconds** looking for them. To make it to training on time he had to run back at **twice** his walking speed.

Below is an incomplete **distance-time graph** for Steve's journey.

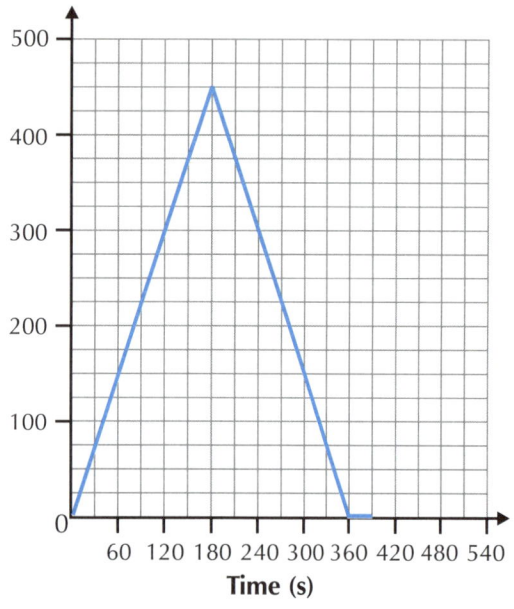

a) How long did it take Steve to walk to training?

....

b) How far away from the training ground does Steve live?

....

c) Complete the graph to show Steve's run back from his house to training (with his boots).

Steve ran back at twice his walking pace, so the journey must have taken half the time of the first one.

Q5 A train travels from point **A** to point **B** in **10 minutes**.

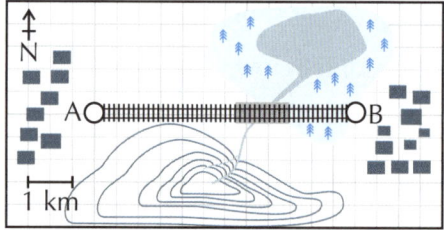

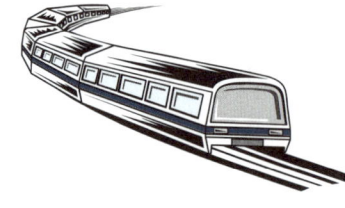

Are the following statements **true** or **false**?

                                                           True False

a) The train's average velocity is 0.6 m/s due east.

b) The train's average speed is 0.6 m/s.

c) The train's average speed is 10 m/s.

d) The train's average velocity is 60 m/s due east.

Don't forget to check your units.

Top Tips: Remember, speed and velocity are basically the **same thing** (they're measured in the same way...) — it's just that when you talk about velocity you've got to give a **direction**. As for all those distance-time graphs, they're not too hard once you've practised, so make sure you've got these ones right, and if you're still unsure, check up on all the facts and try again.

Module P4 — Explaining Motion

Velocity

Q1 Describe the **type of motion** happening at each of the labelled points on the velocity-time graph.

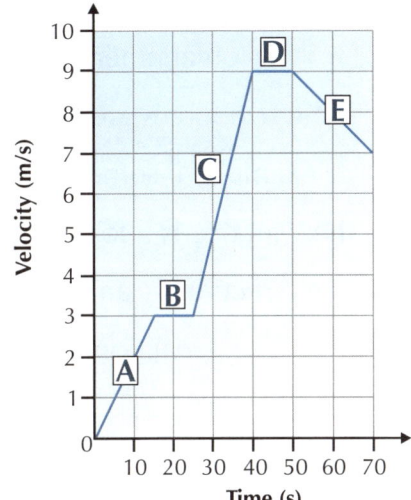

A ....

B ....

C ....

D ....

E ....

Q2 The **monorail** at Buffers' Theme Park takes people from the visitor centre to the main park and back again. It travels at the same **speed** on the outward and return journeys.

The monorail's velocity on the outward journey is 12 m/s. What is its velocity on the return journey?

....

Q3 The distance-time graph and the velocity-time graph below both indicate the **same** three journeys.

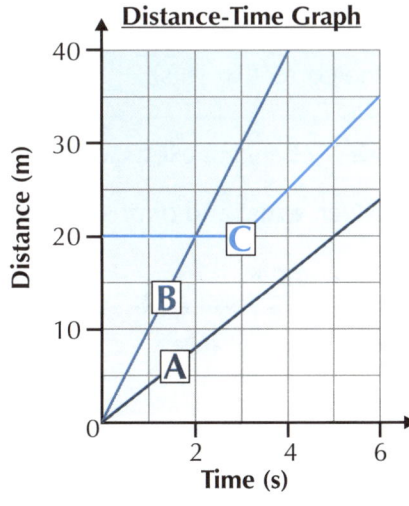 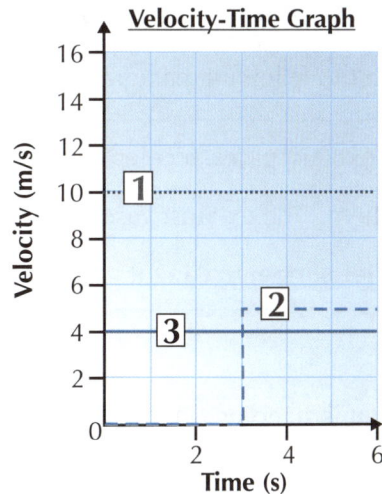

Draw lines to show how the distance-time and velocity-time graphs match up.

Line A   Line 1

Line B   Line 2

Line C   Line 3

Module P4 — Explaining Motion

Forces and Friction

Q1 Complete the following passage.

When an object exerts a .... on another object, it experiences a force in return. The two forces are called an .... pair. For example, if someone leans on a wall with a force of 150 N, the wall exerts a force of .... N in the opposite direction — an '.................... and ....' reaction.

Q2 On the way down a slide, a penguin experiences friction.

a) Between which two objects is friction acting?

....

b) On the picture, label the direction in which friction is acting on the penguin.

c) Suggest how the penguin could reduce friction to speed up his slide.

....

Q3 A **jet engine** uses air to burn fuel, producing **exhaust** gases which accelerate backwards from the rear of the engine.

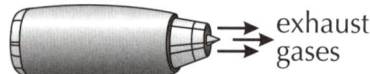

Complete the following paragraph by circling the correct word(s).

The exhaust gases accelerate because the **air / jet engine** exerts **a force / friction** on them. The exhaust gases exert **a greater / an equal** and opposite force on the **air / jet engine**, making it move **forwards / backwards**.

Q4 A **flamingo** is standing on one leg.

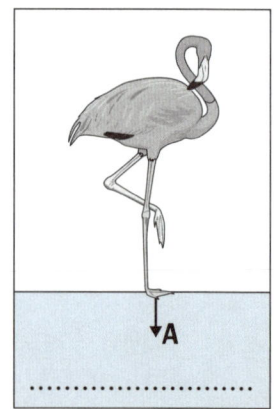

a) Label the force A shown on the diagram.

b) Add a labelled arrow B to show the other force in the interaction pair.

c) Complete the following sentences about the two forces:

Force A is exerted by the .... on the .... Force B is exerted by the .... on the ....

Forces and Motion

Q1 A teapot sits on a table.

a) Complete the sentence below by circling the correct words.

The weight of the teapot is **greater than / balanced by / less than** a reaction **force / friction** from the table.

b) Jane picks up the teapot and hangs it from the ceiling by a rope. What vertical forces now act on the teapot?

....

c) The rope breaks and the teapot accelerates towards the floor. Are the vertical forces balanced?

....

Q2 A bear rides a bike north at a constant speed.

a) Label the forces acting on the bear.

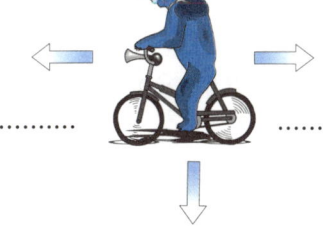

b) The bear brakes and slows down. Are the forces balanced **as** he slows down? If not, which direction is the resultant force in?

....

Q3 The diagram on the right shows the **forces** acting on an aeroplane.

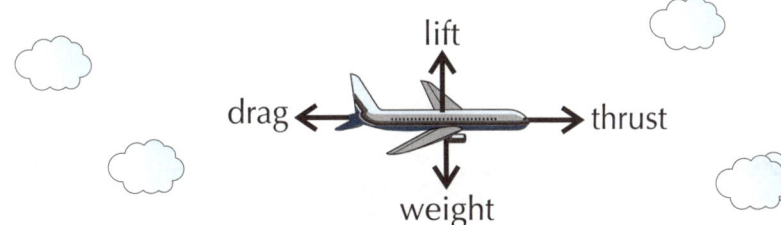

a) The aircraft is flying horizontally at a constant speed of 200 m/s. Which of the following statements about the aeroplane is true? Circle the appropriate letter.

    A   The thrust is bigger than the drag and the lift is bigger than the weight.

    B   The thrust is smaller than the drag and the lift is equal to the weight.

    C   The thrust is equal to the drag and the lift is bigger than the weight.

    D   The thrust is equal to the drag and the lift is equal to the weight.

b) What happens to the forces as the plane descends for landing and slows down to 100 m/s? Choose the correct options to complete the following statements:

    i)   The thrust is **greater than / less than / equal to** the drag.

    ii)   The lift is **greater than / less than / equal to** the weight.

Remember — the plane is losing height as well as slowing down.

Module P4 — Explaining Motion

Forces and Motion

Q4 The **force diagram** on the right shows a train pulling out of a station.

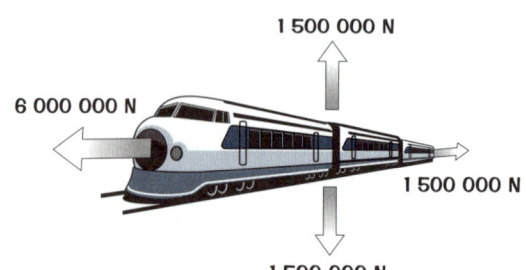

Calculate the resultant force acting on the train in the following directions:

a) Vertical: .... b) Horizontal: ....

Q5 Khaleeda helps Jenny investigate falling objects. Jenny lets go of a tennis ball and Khaleeda times how long it takes to fall. Khaleeda draws the distance-time graph — it looks like the one shown.

Which phrase below describes points X, Y and Z?

Draw a line to match each letter to the correct statement.

    forces in balance

    reaction force from ground acts

    unbalanced force of gravity

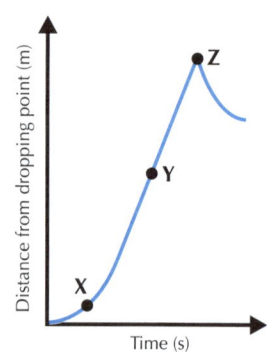

Hint — at X the speed of the tennis ball is increasing.

Q6 Place the following four trucks in order of increasing momentum.

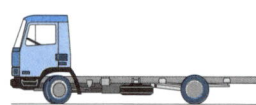       

Truck A	Truck B	Truck C	Truck D
speed = 30 m/s	speed = 10 m/s	speed = 20 m/s	speed = 15 m/s
mass = 3000 kg	mass = 4500 kg	mass = 4000 kg	mass = 3500 kg

....

....

(lowest momentum) .... , ... , ... , ... (highest momentum)

Top Tips: The main thing to remember about momentum (apart from the equation) is that it **changes** when a resultant force acts on an object. So if truck A started to brake, there'd be a resultant backwards force, and the truck's momentum would decrease. Makes perfect sense really.

Module P4 — Explaining Motion

Forces and Motion

Q7 A boat was travelling through the water in a straight line at constant speed. A wave hit the side of the boat, exerting a resultant force of **8000 N** for **1.2 seconds**.

a) Write down the equation that relates force, time and change in momentum.

....

b) Calculate the resulting change in the boat's momentum.

....

....

c) A few minutes later, the boat was hit by another wave. The boat's **change** in momentum was roughly **the same** as last time, but the force of the wave acted over a **shorter time**.

Was the average force acting on the boat during the second wave larger, equal to, or smaller than the average force of the first wave? ....

Q8 Modern cars are equipped with many **safety features** that reduce the **forces** acting on passengers during a collision.

a) Fill in the gaps in the passage below on how seat belts work.

A seat belt .... the time taken to stop a person in a collision. This .... the forces acting on the person, reducing their chances of serious injury.

b) Give **two** other car safety features that work in a similar way.

....

Q9 A **1200 kg car** is travelling at **30 m/s** along the motorway. It crashes into the barrier of the central reservation and is stopped in a period of **1.2 seconds**. Parts of the car body **crumple** in the collision.

a) Find the momentum of the car before the crash.

....

b) Which of the following statements is true? Circle the letter next to the correct answer.

A The car body is designed to crumple to bring the car to a stop as quickly as possible.

B Most cars are designed not to crumple to increase the collision time.

C Car bodies are designed to crumple to increase the collision time.

Module P4 — Explaining Motion

Work

Q1 Circle the correct words to make the following sentences true.

   a) Work involves the transfer of force / heat / **energy**.

   b) To do work a **force** / push acts over a **distance** / time.

   c) Work is measured in watts / **joules**.

Q2 Indicate whether the following statements are true or false.

		True	False
a)	Work is done when a toy car is pushed along the ground.	☐	☐
b)	No work is done if a force is applied to an object which does not move.	☐	☐
c)	Gravity does work on an apple that is not moving.	☐	☐
d)	Gravity does work on an apple that falls out of a tree.	☐	☐

Q3 An elephant exerts a constant force of **1200 N** to push a donkey along a track at a steady 1 m/s.

   a) Calculate the work done by the elephant if the donkey moves **8 m**.
   ....

   b) From where does the elephant get the energy to do this work? ....

   c) Into what form(s) is this energy transferred when work is done on the donkey?
   ....

Q4 Ben's weight is 600 N. He climbs a ladder. The rungs of the ladder are 20 cm apart.

   a) What force is Ben doing work **against** as he climbs?
   ....

   b) How much work does Ben do when he climbs **10 rungs**?
   (Ignore any 'wasted' energy.)
   ....
   ....

Top Tips: Pretty much every 'work done' question you'll come across talks about moving something horizontally. Moving something vertically is exactly the same in principle though — you're just applying a force (at least equivalent to the object's weight) to move the object upwards.

Module P4 — Explaining Motion

Kinetic Energy

Q1 Complete the following sentences by circling the correct word.

a) If the mass of a moving object is doubled, its kinetic energy is halved / **doubled** / quadrupled.

b) If the speed of a moving object is doubled, its kinetic energy is halved / doubled / **quadrupled**.

Q2 Find the **kinetic energy** of a 200 kg tiger running at a speed of 9 m/s.

....

....

Q3 Number the following vehicles 1-3, where 1 is the vehicle carrying the most energy due to its motion, and 3 is the vehicle carrying the least energy.

60 000 kg, 5 m/s   100 kg, 8 m/s   1200 kg, 20 m/s

....

Q4 Jack is riding his bicycle along at a steady speed. His dad gives him a push, doing **50 J** of work on the bicycle and making it speed up.

a) What effect does the push have on Jack's dad and the bicycle?
Tick the boxes next to any correct answers.

☐ The pushing force does work on the bicycle and increases its kinetic energy.

☐ The pushing force doesn't do any work on the bicycle because it was already moving.

☐ The bicycle does work on Jack's dad and increases his kinetic energy.

b) Assuming there is no friction or air resistance, which of the following statements are true?

☐ Jack and his bicycle lose 50 J of kinetic energy.

☐ Jack and his bicycle gain 50 J of kinetic energy.

☐ Jack's dad loses 50 J of energy.

Module P4 — Explaining Motion

Gravitational Potential Energy

Q1 Mike has bought some dumb-bells to help him get buff. He has one **5 kg** weight and one **10 kg** weight stored on the same shelf.

a) Which dumb-bell has more potential energy? Circle the correct answer.

b) Mike moves the 10 kg dumb-bell to a lower shelf. What happens to its potential energy? Circle the correct answer.   *increases / decreases / stays the same*

Q2 Fred works at a DIY shop. He has to load **28** flagstones onto the delivery truck. Each flagstone weighs **250 N** and has to be lifted **1.2 m** onto the truck.

a) How much gravitational potential energy does one flagstone gain when lifted onto the truck? Underline the correct answer.

   300 J   208 J   3000 J

b) What is the **total gravitational potential energy** gained by the flagstones after they are all loaded onto the truck?

....

c) How much **work** does Fred do loading the truck?

....

Q3 A roller coaster and its passengers are stationary at the top of a ride. At this point they have a gravitational potential energy of **300 kJ**. The full roller coaster has a mass of **750 kg**.

a) Draw lines to connect the correct energy statement with each stage of the roller coaster.

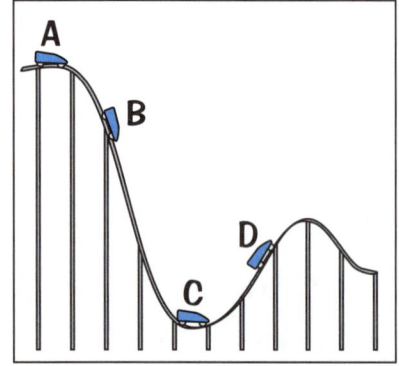

A   minimum G.P.E., maximum K.E.

B   K.E. is being converted to G.P.E.

C   maximum G.P.E.

D   G.P.E. is being converted to K.E.

b) i) When the roller coaster is at half its original height, how much **kinetic energy** should it have?

....

ii) Explain why in real life the kinetic energy is **less** than this.

....

....

Module P4 — Explaining Motion

Gravitational Potential Energy

Q4 A toy cricket ball hit straight upwards has a gravitational potential energy of **121 J** at the **top** of its flight.

What is the ball's **kinetic energy** just before it hits the ground? Tick the box next to the correct answer.

☐ 242 J   ☐ 0 J   ☐ 121 J

Q5 Jo weighs **500 N**. She is sitting at the top of a helter-skelter ride.

a) At the top of the helter-skelter, Jo is **8 m** above the ground. What is her gravitational potential energy?

....

b) Jo comes down the helter-skelter and at the bottom her kinetic energy is **1500 J**. How much **energy** has been 'wasted' in coming down the ride?

....

c) Which **force(s)** cause this energy to be wasted?

....

Q6 A skier with a weight of **700 N** rides a chairlift to a point **20 m** higher up a ski slope. She then skis back down to the **same height** as she got on the chairlift.

a) Calculate the **work done** by the chairlift in carrying the skier up the slope.

....

....

b) Assuming no energy is wasted, how much kinetic energy does the skier gain by skiing down the slope?

....

....

Top Tips: Kinetic energy, gravitational potential energy, work done... they're all measured in joules, so they're all energy. If you 'do work' on something, you're converting energy — by exerting a force on the object which makes it move. If you start an object moving or make it speed up you've given it some K.E. If you move the object away from the ground, you've given it some G.P.E.

Module P4 — Explaining Motion

Bungee Jumping

Q1 Read the passage below and answer the questions that follow.

Bungee jumping is a popular sport and recreational activity, carefully managed to minimise the risks. Millions of jumps have been successfully and safely completed around the world, with the highest commercial jump now standing at 233 m (764 ft) in Macau, China.

A bungee jumper at the Macau jump starts on the 233 m high platform, then gains speed for 5 seconds before the pull of the bungee cord begins to affect their freefall, as shown on the graph.

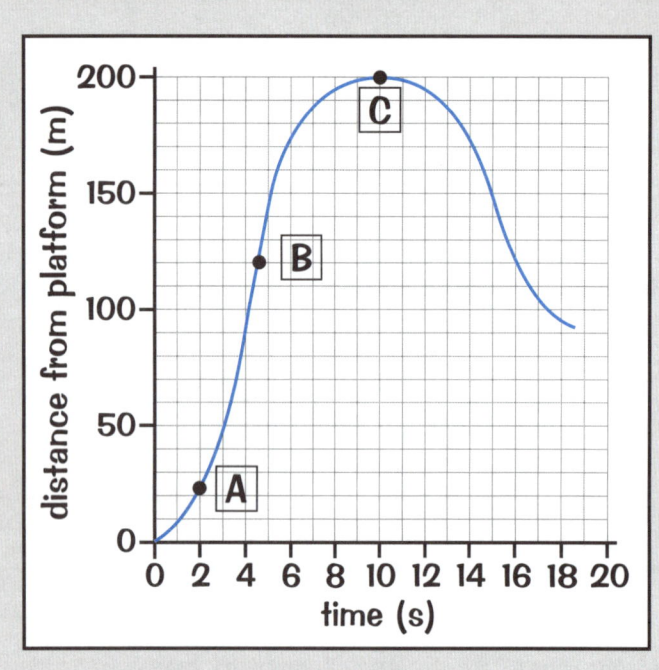

After 10 seconds they come to within 30 m or so of the ground before rebounding upwards. Jumpers can reach speeds of up to 200 km/h.

A common misconception about the dangers of bungee jumping is the idea that the cord may snap. Bungee cord is made from a tightly wound matrix of extremely strong elastic fibres, and most cords can hold up to 1000 kg before snapping.

The most common cause of bungee accidents is thought to be overestimation of the length of bungee cord needed. People expect the cord to slow the jumper down as soon as it reaches its natural length (the length of the cord when nothing is suspended from it), but this is not the case — at its natural length, the cord has virtually no resistance, and the jumper carries on gaining speed for some time before they are slowed down. The cords used at Macau have a natural length of 50 m.

a) Using the distance-time graph in the passage, describe the motion of the jumper at:

i) point B .... ii) point C ....

b) i) Which of the following are forces that act **vertically** on the jumper at point C? Underline your answer(s).

   gravity   kinetic energy   tension   mass   potential energy

ii) Which of the forces you have underlined is the greatest at point C? ....

Module P4 — Explaining Motion

Bungee Jumping

c) How many times longer than its natural length is the bungee cord at point C?
Tick the box next to the correct answer.

☐ 2 times   ☐ 3 times   ☐ 4 times   ☐ 5 times

d) According to the distance-time graph, a jumper typically travels **200 m** in **10 s** during the initial descent. Calculate the typical jumper's average speed during this time.

....

e) The graph below is for the first 13 seconds of a jump at Macau.

If the jumper's mass was **75 kg**, what would be the jumper's **momentum** at his top speed?

....

f) After his jump, a jumper weighing **950 N** climbs back up to the start point, a vertical distance of **233 m**. Calculate the work he does during this climb.

....

g) Skydivers reach speeds similar to those of bungee jumpers. By streamlining their shape, they can reach around 90 m/s (about 200 mph). However, they struggle to go any faster than this, no matter how long they're falling for. Suggest why.

Think about the vertical forces acting on them at constant speed...

....

....

....

Module P4 — Explaining Motion

DNA — Making Proteins

Q1 Tick the boxes to show whether the following statements are **true** or **false**.

    True False

a) Genes are sections of DNA that code for specific proteins. ☐ ☐

b) Each cell contains different genes, which is why we have different types of cell. ☐ ☐

c) Proteins are made at ribosomes. ☐ ☐

d) Nucleotides are made up of chains of DNA. ☐ ☐

Q2 The following questions are about **DNA**.

a) What is the function of DNA?

....

b) What name is given to the shape of a DNA molecule? Circle the correct answer.

    single helix   double helix   triple helix

c) How many different bases make up the DNA structure? ....

Q3 Complete the lower sequence of bases on the section of **DNA** shown below.

```
A G G C T A G C C A A T C G C C G A A G C T C A
| | | | | | | | | | | | | | | | | | | | | | | |
T C C G A T C G G T T A G C G
```

Q4 Complete the passage using words from the box below.
Some words may be used more than once.

| nucleotide | cytoplasm | nucleus | messenger | ribosomes |

Proteins are produced by organelles called ...., which are found in the .... of a cell. Information from DNA needs to get to the .... but the DNA's too large to leave the .... A copy of the gene is made which acts as a .... between the DNA and the ....

Cell Division — Mitosis

Q1 Tick the boxes to show whether the following statements are **true** or **false**.

		True	False
a)	During cell growth the number of organelles increases.	☐	☐
b)	Chromosomes are found in the cytoplasm of an animal cell.	☐	☐
c)	Before a cell divides by mitosis, it duplicates its DNA.	☐	☐
d)	Mitosis is where a cell divides to create two genetically identical copies.	☐	☐
e)	Organisms divide by mitosis in order to grow.	☐	☐
f)	Organisms do not use mitosis to replace damaged cells.	☐	☐

Q2 Complete the following passage using the words below.

splits   different   nucleotides   chromosomes   identical   grows

Before a cell splits in two by mitosis, the cell .... and the DNA contained within the cell is copied. To copy ...., the molecule of DNA ...., then new strands form alongside the old ones. So two DNA molecules that are .... to the original one are formed.

Q3 The following diagram shows the different stages of **mitosis**. Circle the correct word(s) in each pair to give a description of the different stages.

a) The cell has **two** / **three** copies of its DNA all spread out in long strings.

b) The DNA forms **X** / **M** shaped chromosomes.

c) The chromosomes line up at the **edge** / **centre** of the cell. **Cell fibres** / **Ribosomes** pull them apart.

d) Membranes form around each set of chromosomes, forming the **nuclei** / **cytoplasm** of the new cells.

e) The **cytoplasm** / **chromosome** divides to form two new cells.

Module B5 — Growth and Development

Cell Division — Meiosis

Q1 Tick the boxes below to show which statements are true of **mitosis**, **meiosis** or **both**.

		Mitosis	Meiosis
a)	Halves the number of chromosomes.	☐	☐
b)	Chromosomes line up in the centre of the cell.	☐	☐
c)	Forms cells that are genetically different.	☐	☐
d)	In humans, it only happens in the reproductive organs.	☐	☐

Q2 Draw lines to match the descriptions of the stage of **meiosis** to the right diagram below. The first one has been done for you.

a) ——— The pairs are pulled apart, so each new cell only has one copy of each type of chromosome.

b) Before the cell starts to divide it duplicates its DNA to produce an exact copy.

c) There are now four gametes, each containing half the original number of chromosomes.

d) For the first meiotic division the chromosomes line up in their pairs across the centre of the cell.

e) The chromosomes line up across the centre of the cell ready for the second division, and the left and right arms are pulled apart.

Q3 During sexual reproduction, two **gametes** combine to form a new individual.

Use words from the box below to complete the following passage.

| zygote | bases | full | fertilisation | half | chromosomes | twice |

Gametes have .... the usual number of .... so that when two gametes join together during .... the resulting .... will have the .... number of chromosomes.

Module B5 — Growth and Development

Development from a Single Cell

Q1 Tick the correct boxes to show whether the following statements are **true** or **false**.

		True	False
a)	Cells in an early embryo are unspecialised.	☐	☐
b)	Blood cells are undifferentiated.	☐	☐
c)	Nerve cells are specialised cells.	☐	☐
d)	Adult stem cells are as versatile as embryonic stem cells.	☐	☐
e)	Stem cells in bone marrow can differentiate into any type of cell.	☐	☐

Q2 The following terms are related to **stem cells**. Say what each of the following terms mean.

a) differentiation ....
....

b) undifferentiated cells ....
....

Q3 Complete the following passage about stem cells by using words from the box.

twelve	proteins	eight	active	six	genes

In humans, all the cells in the embryo are undifferentiated up to the .... cell stage. What type of cell a stem cell differentiates into depends on what .... are .... in that cell — and so what .... that cell produces.

Q4 Circle the cell types below that are **specialised**.

differentiated cell   gamete   red blood cell

embryonic stem cell   nerve cell   adult stem cells

Q5 How are **embryonic** stem cells different from **adult** stem cells?

....
....
....

Top Tips: Stem cells are cutting-edge stuff right now. You'll probably see loads more of them in the news in the future as scientists use them to try to find new cures for disorders like Parkinson's.

Module B5 — Growth and Development

Growth in Plants

Q1 Put the following parts of a plant into the correct column in the table to show whether they are plant tissues or organs.

flowers   phloem   xylem   roots   leaves

Organs	Tissues

Q2 Tick the boxes to show whether the following statements are **true** or **false**.

    True False

a) Plant shoots grow away from light.

b) Plant roots grow towards light.

c) Positive phototropism ensures that roots grow deep into the soil for nutrients.

d) If the tip of a shoot is removed, the shoot may stop growing.

Q3 Sally takes **two cuttings** from her favourite plant and tries to **grow both** using rooting powder to produce new plants. One cutting grows **well** but the other **doesn't**. The two cuttings are shown in the diagram below. Cutting 2 includes a bud.

a) What is a 'cutting'?

....

b) What does rooting powder contain that helps cuttings to grow?

....

c) Will the new plants be clones of each other?

....

d) Which of the cuttings shown would you expect to **grow best**, and why?

....

....

....

cutting 1

cutting 2

Module B5 — Growth and Development

Growth in Plants

Q4 Give two differences in **growth** between plants and animals.

1. ....

2. ....

Q5 **Phototropism** is necessary for the survival of plants. Complete the following passage using words from the box. Some words may be used more than once.

| nutrients | light | sound | sunlight |
| towards | away | direction | |

Positive phototropism is growth .... a ....
source. Negative phototropism is growth .... from a
.... source. Plants need .... and water
from the ground and .... to grow. Phototropism allows plants
to grow in the right .... to get these things.

Q6 Tick the boxes to show whether the following statements are **true** or **false**.   True   False

a) Meristem tissue at the tips of stems contains the plant equivalent of adult stem cells.

b) The cells in the meristem lose their properties as the plant ages.

c) Meristem tissue is generated in the stem of the plant and transported to the roots and shoots where it is needed for growth.

d) Cells produced by dividing meristem cells can differentiate to become cells in flowers.

e) Differentiation is triggered by turning certain genes on or off.

f) Cells behind the meristem tissue grow via cell elongation.

Top Tips: Phototropism is incredibly useful to plants. In fact, without it plants would probably have roots and shoots just anywhere — it wouldn't be too efficient trying to harness light energy whilst deep in the dark soil, with all those worms.

Module B5 — Growth and Development

Stem Cells and Parkinson's

Q1 Read the passage about using **stem cells** to treat **Parkinson's**, then answer the questions that follow.

> Stem cells have been one of the decade's hottest research topics, but have so far not lived up to their promise of being a wonder-cure. However, there have recently been promising results from studies using adult stem cells to treat Parkinson's disease.
>
> Symptoms of Parkinson's disease include shaking movements, muscle stiffness and difficulty in moving. Parkinson's can also cause problems with handwriting, speech and balance, leaving many sufferers with a poor quality of life.
>
> The symptoms of Parkinson's are caused by the death of nerve cells that produce a chemical called dopamine. Dopamine carries signals in the parts of the brain controlling movement — as the levels decline, sufferers' ability to control their movements decreases.
>
> A recent study of a new treatment showed that adult stem cells could be made to differentiate to replace the dead dopamine-producing nerve cells. The stem cells were removed from a healthy area of each patient's brain and implanted into the area damaged by Parkinson's. Once transplanted, the nerve cells began to differentiate into dopamine-producing cells as hoped. However, the cells then started to die. Unless this death of the new cells can be prevented this treatment is not a permanent cure.
>
> These studies show that more research is needed to realise the potential of stem cells, and that they may well provide a cure for Parkinson's and other diseases in the future.

a) Give **three** common symptoms of Parkinson's disease.

....

b) What was the key **problem** found in the human study using adult stem cells to treat Parkinson's? Circle the correct answer.

- The patients' immune systems rejected the implanted stem cells.
- The stem cells died soon after they were transplanted into the patients' brains.
- The stem cells didn't differentiate into the right kind of nerve cell.
- The scientists had great difficulty collecting healthy stem cells.

c) Explain how replacing dead dopamine-producing nerve cells in patients with Parkinson's could reduce symptoms such as shaking.

....

....

Module B5 — Growth and Development

Chemicals in the Atmosphere

Q1 The table shows some of the **gases** that are found in **dry air**. Complete the table to show whether the gases are elements or compounds, and give their **chemical symbols**.

substance	element or compound	chemical symbol
oxygen		
carbon dioxide		
argon		
nitrogen		

Q2 Use the words in the box to complete the passage below.

molecular	compounds	weak	metallic
atoms	non-metallic		strong

Most non-metallic elements and most compounds formed from .... elements are .... substances. The .... within the molecules are held together by very .... covalent bonds. The forces of attraction between the molecules are very ....

Q3 Complete the following sentences by circling the correct option.

a) The melting and boiling points of simple molecular substances are **low / high**.

b) Simple molecular substances **conduct / don't conduct** electricity.

c) Simple molecular substances are usually **gases and liquids / solids** at room temperature.

Top Tips: There are loads of gases floating around in our atmosphere. You need to understand how their structure gives them their physical properties, like low boiling and melting points and low electrical conductivity.

Chemicals in the Hydrosphere

Q1 Choose from the words in the box to complete the passage below.

> molecules   salty   dissolved   water
> ions   salts   gases
>
> The Earth's hydrosphere consists of all the .... on the Earth's
> surface and the compounds .... in it. Many of these compounds
> are ...., which are made up of .... This is why
> seawater is described as being ....

Q2 Sodium chloride has an **ionic structure**.

Circle the correct words to explain why sodium chloride has a high melting point.

> Sodium chloride has very **strong / weak** chemical bonds between the
> **negative / positive** sodium ions and the **negative / positive** chloride ions.
> This means that it needs a **little / large** amount of energy to break the bonds.

Q3 Potassium chloride is an example of a **salt** found in the **sea**. Mike carries out an experiment to find out if **potassium chloride** conducts electricity. He tests the compound when it's **solid** and when it's **dissolved** in water.

a) Complete the following table of results.

	Conducts electricity?
When solid	
When dissolved in water	

b) Explain why there is a difference between the conductivity of an ionic compound in solution and its conductivity as a solid.

....

....

....

Module C5 — Chemicals of the Natural Environment

Chemicals in the Lithosphere

Q1 Choose from the words in the box to complete the passage describing the Earth's **lithosphere**.

> minerals aluminium mantle silicon
> elements argon crust oxygen
>
> The .... and part of the .... just below it make
> up the Earth's lithosphere. It mostly consists of a mixture of ....
> ...., ... and .... are
> .... found in large amounts in the crust.

Q2 An **abundant** compound in the Earth's lithosphere is **silicon dioxide**.

a) Why does silicon dioxide have a high melting and boiling point?

....

....

b) Explain why silicon dioxide doesn't conduct electricity.

....

c) State another property of silicon dioxide.

....

d) Give **two** types of rock in which silicon dioxide is found in **large quantities**.

....

Q3 Circle the correct words to complete the following paragraph.

> Giant covalent structures contain **charged ions** / **uncharged atoms**.
> The covalent bonds between the atoms are **strong** / **weak**.
> Giant covalent structures have **high** / **low** melting points,
> they usually **do** / **don't** conduct electricity and they are
> usually **soluble** / **insoluble** in water.

The results suggest a giant covalent structure.

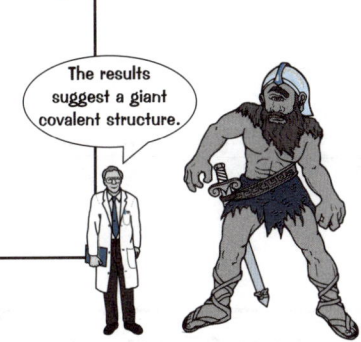

Top Tips: It seems to be all spheres in this section — the atmosphere, the hydrosphere, the lithosphere... Make sure you don't get the facts about them all muddled up. You don't want to be putting the fish up in the sky, or clouds down below the Earth's surface...

Module C5 — Chemicals of the Natural Environment

Chemicals in the Lithosphere

Q4 The tables below show the **percentage composition** of samples of two different types of **rock**. One rock is limestone (mostly calcium carbonate) and the other is sandstone (mostly silicon dioxide).

Decide which sample is **limestone** and which sample is **sandstone**, and explain your answers.

Sample A	% composition
Si	44.0
O	51.0
Al	0.8
Ca	0.7
Mg	0.1
Other	3.4

Sample B	% composition
Si	1.3
O	47.1
Al	1.6
Ca	38.5
C	11.0
Mg	0.5

Look at the main components of each rock.

Sample A is: ....

Reason: ....

Sample B is: ....

Reason: ....

Q5 Some **minerals** (e.g. diamond) are very valuable as **gemstones**.

a) Explain why some minerals are used as gemstones.
   ....

b) Why are some gemstones so **valuable**?
   ....

c) Explain why diamond has a high melting point.
   ....
   ....

Top Tips: Examiners just love setting data interpretation questions, and this topic is as good as any for finding one. You might have to interpret data about the amounts of elements in different types of rock, or you might have to apply your knowledge of giant covalent structures to other substances with this type of structure (such as diamond).

Module C5 — Chemicals of the Natural Environment

Chemicals in the Biosphere

Q1 List **six elements** that all **living things** contain.

1. ....
2. ....
3. ....
4. ....
5. ....
6. ....

Q2 The diagram shows the **structural formula** of a **carbohydrate** molecule. List the **elements** it contains and write its **molecular formula**.

Elements ....

Molecular formula ....

Q3 The diagram shows the **nitrogen cycle**, which describes how the element nitrogen moves between the different spheres of the earth.

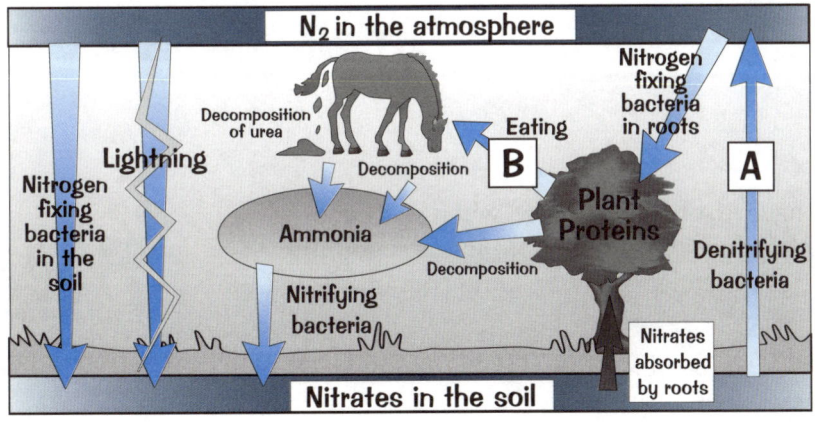

Tick the boxes to show what the labelled arrows represent.

a) Arrow **A** represents:

Denitrifying bacteria moving from the soil to the atmosphere. ☐

Denitrifying bacteria converting nitrates in the soil into nitrogen in the atmosphere. ☐

b) Arrow **B** represents:

Nitrogen from plants moving into animals by feeding. ☐

Nitrogen being released into the atmosphere through feeding. ☐

Module C5 — Chemicals of the Natural Environment

Metals from Minerals

Q1 Tick the boxes to show whether each of the statements below are **true** or **false**.

		True	False
a)	Ores are rocks containing minerals from which metals can be extracted.	☐	☐
b)	The more reactive the metal, the easier it is to extract from its ore.	☐	☐
c)	Zinc, iron and copper can all be extracted by heating their ores with carbon monoxide.	☐	☐
d)	When a metal oxide loses oxygen, it is reduced.	☐	☐

Q2 Fill in the blanks in the passage below about **extracting metals** from their **ores**.

> electrolysis   more   carbon   less
> reduction   oxygen   below

.... is often used to extract metals that are .... it in the reactivity series. Oxygen is removed from a metal oxide in a process called .... Other metals have to be extracted using .... because they are .... reactive.

Q3 **Copper** may have first been extracted when someone accidentally dropped some copper ore into a **wood fire**. When the ashes were cleared away some copper was left.

a) Explain how dropping copper ore into a fire could lead to the extraction of copper.

....

b) Why do you think that copper was one of the first metals to be extracted from its ore?

....

Top Tips: Metals aren't usually found in the ground as pure lumps. They need to be extracted from their ores, and this is done by a variety of methods. The ones you need to know about are reduction using carbon and electrolysis. Which is what these pages are all about...

Module C5 — Chemicals of the Natural Environment

Electrolysis

Q1 Complete the passage about **electrolysis** using words from the box below.

| dissolved | molecules | electric | given to |
| decompose | external circuit | taken from | molten |

During the electrolysis of an ionic compound, an .... current is passed through a .... or .... substance, causing it to ....

Electrons are .... ions at the positive electrode and pass through the .... to the negative electrode, where they are .... other ions in the solution.

Atoms or .... are formed at the electrodes.

Q2 The diagram below shows the electrolysis of **molten aluminium oxide**.

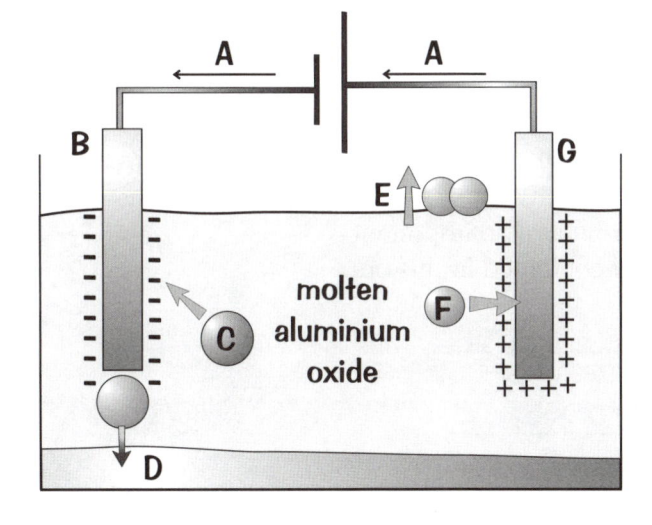

a) Write the letter showing the following:

   i) Anode: ....   iv) Aluminum ion: ....

   ii) Cathode: ....   v) Oxide ion: ....

   iii) Oxygen gas: ....

b) What does A represent?

....

Module C5 — Chemicals of the Natural Environment

Electrolysis

Q3 For electrolysis to work the **electrolyte** needs to be either a **solution** or **molten**. Circle the correct reason why.

For electricity to flow through the electrolyte, the ions need to be in fixed positions.

For electricity to flow through the electrolyte, the ions need to be free to move.

Q4 Tick the correct boxes to show whether the following statements are **true** or **false**.

    True False

a) Ionic substances can only be electrolysed if molten or in solution.

b) In the extraction of aluminium the electrolyte is molten aluminium metal.

c) The aluminium produced is molten.

d) Aluminium ions gain electrons in electrolysis.

e) Aluminium is formed at the positive electrode.

Q5 **Aluminium** is the most **abundant** metal in the Earth's crust.

  a) i) Circle the correct word:

      The most common aluminium ore is bauxite / cryolite.

    ii) Give the name and formula of an important aluminium compound contained in this ore.

      Name ....

      Formula ....

Goodness, how awfully common...

  b) Why can't aluminium be extracted by **reduction** with carbon?

  c) Although it's very common, aluminium was not discovered until about 200 years ago. Suggest why.

Top Tips: Usually, things that are common are cheap to buy — like potatoes. But, even though aluminium is as common a metal as you're going to get, it's not actually that cheap because it costs a lot to extract. (Potatoes, on the other hand, are easy to extract — just get digging.)

Module C5 — Chemicals of the Natural Environment

Metals

Q1 The table shows the **properties** of **four elements** found in the periodic table.

ELEMENT	MELTING POINT (°C)	DENSITY (g/cm³)	ELECTRICAL CONDUCTIVITY
A	1084	8.9	Excellent
B	−39	13.6	Very good
C	3500	3.51	Very poor
D	1536	7.87	Very good

a) Which **three** of the above elements are most likely to be **metals**?

....

b) Which property shows that the other element is **not** a metal?

....

Q2 This table shows some of the **properties** of four different **metals**.

Metal	Heat conduction	Cost	Resistance to corrosion	Strength
1	average	high	excellent	good
2	average	medium	good	excellent
3	excellent	low	good	good
4	low	high	average	poor

Use the information in the table to choose which metal would be **best** for making:

a) Saucepan bases ....

b) Car bodies ....

c) A statue for a town centre ....

Think about how long a statue would have to last for.

Q3 Complete the following sentences about metals.

a) Metals have a giant structure of atoms held together by strong .... bonds.

b) Metals are good conductors of .... and .... because they have lots of free ....

c) The atoms in metals can slide over each other, so metals are ....

Module C5 — Chemicals of the Natural Environment

Environmental Impact

Q1 Metal ores are **finite resources**.

a) Explain what is meant by a 'finite resource', and why relying on finite resources could cause a problem in the future.

....

....

b) Suggest one way to **reduce** this problem.

....

....

Q2 New **mines** always have **social**, **economic** and **environmental** consequences. Complete this table by putting **two** more possible effects of a new mine in each of the columns.

Remember to include both positive and negative effects.

Social	Economic	Environmental
Services, e.g. Healthcare may be improved because of influx of people.		Pollution from traffic.

___

Top Tips: It's important to be able to weigh up the issues surrounding the extraction of metals. There are plenty of positive and negative effects of mining, so make sure you've got them sorted so that you don't have to spend loads of time thinking if they come up in the exam.

Module C5 — Chemicals of the Natural Environment

Environmental Impact

Q3 Read the article below and answer the questions that follow.

Metals play a major role in modern life. However, none of the stages in the life cycle of a metal product are free from environmental problems.

Mining

Although mining brings money and employment, which have a positive impact on the development of an area, there are plenty of negatives. Mining destroys landscapes and habitats, produces waste products and causes noise pollution. Transporting the ore takes energy and causes pollution.

Extraction

Extracting pure metal from the ore is also not without problems. Non-renewable resources, such as fossil fuels, are usually used to provide the energy needed to extract the metals. This in turn leads to air pollution, which brings its own problems such as acid rain and climate change.

Use

Metals are often used for products which have an impact on the environment. Take, for example, cars — they burn non-renewable fuels and produce pollution.

Disposal

At the end of their life, metals are often disposed of in landfill sites. These are unattractive and some metals can be dangerous if disposed of in this way. Vehicles accessing the sites cause pollution, dust and noise.

One answer to these problems is recycling. Take aluminium — it can be recycled over and over again without losing any of its properties in the process. The process doesn't take long either — recycled aluminium cans are usually back on the shelves within eight weeks.

In the UK, it's estimated that we use about 5 billion aluminium cans every year. In 2001, 42% of these cans were recycled (up from 31% of cans used in 1996).

Recycling aluminium uses only 5% of the energy needed to extract pure aluminium from bauxite, and produces only 5% of the carbon dioxide emissions.

For every 1 kg of aluminium recycled, 6 kg of bauxite, 4 kg of chemical products and 14 kWh of electricity are saved. Put another way, 20 recycled cans can be made with the energy it takes to make just one brand new can.

The use of aluminium is rising quickly so it makes sense to encourage people to recycle more aluminium. However, not all areas have good recycling collection services, and some people don't make the effort to separate their recyclable waste. Some people also wonder whether it is 'environmentally friendly' to produce all the plastic boxes used to collect cans from doorsteps.

Module C5 — Chemicals of the Natural Environment

Environmental Impact

a) Give two **environmental problems** associated with the mining of metal ores.
   ....
   ....

b) Describe one **benefit** that an aluminium ore mine can have for the local area.
   ....

c) How can the use of metals cause environmental problems **indirectly**?
   ....

d) The article states that about 5 billion aluminium cans are used every year in the UK.

   1 billion = 1 000 000 000

   i) Approximately how many cans were **recycled** in **1996**?
      ....

   ii) Approximately how many cans were **recycled** in **2001**?
       ....

   iii) How many more cans were recycled in 2001 compared to 1996?
        ....

e) State **two** reasons that people might give for not recycling their aluminium packaging.
   ....
   ....
   ....

f) Select one sentence or phrase from the article that demonstrates that recycling aluminium is very energy efficient.
   ....
   ....

Module C5 — Chemicals of the Natural Environment

Module P5 — Electric Circuits

Static Electricity

Q1 Fill in the gaps in these sentences with the words below.

> electrons   positive   static   friction   insulating   negative
>
> .... electricity can build up when two .... materials are rubbed together. The .... causes .... to be transferred from one material onto the other. This leaves a .... charge on one of the materials and a .... charge on the other.

Q2 **Circle** the pairs of charges that would attract each other and **underline** those that would repel.

positive and positive   positive and negative   negative and positive   negative and negative

Q3 Tick the boxes to show whether the following statements are **true** or **false**.   True   False

a) Electrons are negatively charged particles. ☐ ☐

b) Areas of positive charge are caused by the movement of positive charges. ☐ ☐

c) Negatively charged areas occur because electrons are attracted to each other. ☐ ☐

Q4 Two friends are talking about some of the **effects** of static electricity.

Sara: Why is the TV screen always dusty — my mum cleans it all the time?

Lisa: Why does my hair sometimes stick out and cling to the brush?

Circle the correct word(s) from each pair to complete the answers to their questions.

> **Lisa:** Static electricity can build up when you brush your hair. Each strand of hair develops the **same / opposite** charge, so they all **attract / repel** each other. The hairbrush develops the opposite charge, so your hair is **attracted to / repelled by** it.
>
> **Sara:** When Sara's mum cleans the TV screen she causes a **removal / build-up** of static electricity on it. Dust particles are attracted to the **charged / neutral** TV screen.

Top Tips: Static electricity's responsible for many of life's little irritations — bad hair days, those little shocks you get from touching car doors, the crackling noises you get from jumpers...

Electric Current

Q1 Circle the correct word from each pair to complete the following sentences.

a) Current is the production / **flow** of **charge** / energy around a circuit.

b) **Voltage** / Resistance acts like a force that **pushes** / pulls the current round the circuit.

c) Voltage / **Resistance** restricts the flow of current round the circuit.

Q2 Connect each **quantity** with the name and symbol of its **unit**.

Symbol	Quantity	Unit
A	Current	volts
V	Resistance	amperes
Ω	Voltage	ohms

Q3 Tick the boxes to show whether the following statements are **true** or **false**.

	True	False
a) Conventional current flows from negative to positive.	☐	☐
b) A component (such as a lamp or motor) resists the flow of charge through it.	☐	☐
c) Electrons flow from negative to positive.	☐	☐
d) The wires in an electric circuit are full of negative charges that cannot move.	☐	☐

Q4 The flow of electricity in circuits can be compared to the flow of **water in pipes**.

a) Draw lines to connect the labelled parts of a water circuit with the corresponding parts of an electrical circuit.

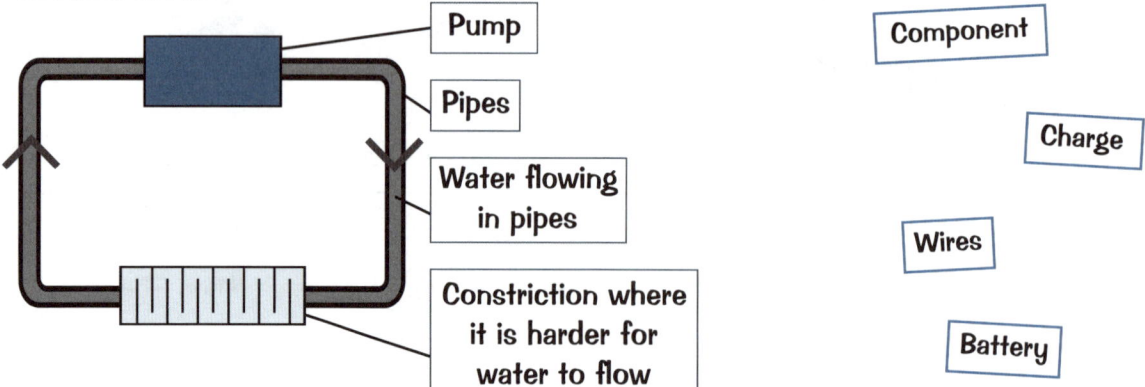

Water circuit labels: Pump, Pipes, Water flowing in pipes, Constriction where it is harder for water to flow

Electrical circuit labels: Component, Charge, Wires, Battery

b) The pump in the water circuit is turned up. What would the equivalent action be in an electrical circuit? Circle the correct answer.

Increasing the **current** of the power supply

Increasing the **resistance** of the power supply

Increasing the **voltage** of the power supply

Module P5 — Electric Circuits

Electric Current

Q5 The **current** that flows in a circuit depends on the **voltage** of the power supply and the **resistance** of the components.

a) Circle the correct word from each pair in the sentence below.

Increasing the resistance / **voltage** of the battery increases the 'push' on the **charge** / components, so **increases** / decreases the current.

b) How should the total resistance of a circuit be changed in order to:

i) increase the current? ....

ii) decrease the current? ....

Q6 **Electrical wires** are usually made of copper and covered in an **insulating** material.

a) Draw lines to connect each material with its electrical property and the reason for this property.

Plastic   Insulator   Material contains lots of charges that are free to move.

Metal   Conductor   Charges within material are mostly fixed in position.

b) What charged particles move when current flows in a copper wire?

....

Q7 Ranjit closes the switch in the **electric circuit** shown and the **lamp lights** up. When Ranjit **opens** the switch the lamp **goes out**. He discusses why this happens with his friends.

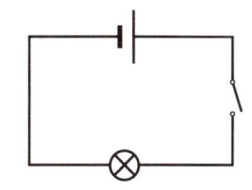

Lara says, "When the switch is open, charge leaks out and so doesn't reach the lamp."

Brian says, "All the charge must have been used up when the switch was closed."

Ranjit says, "The circuit is not complete when the switch is open so no current flows."

a) Who has the correct explanation? ....

b) Explain what's wrong with the other two explanations.

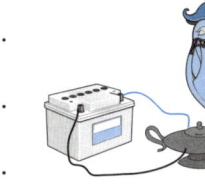

....

....

....

....

Module P5 — Electric Circuits

Circuits — The Basics

Q1 Match up these items from a standard test circuit with the **correct description** and **symbol**. The first one has been done for you.

ITEM	DESCRIPTION	SYMBOL
Cell	Provides the 'push' on the charge.	—(A)—
Variable Resistor	The item you're testing.	—(variable resistor)—
Component	Used to alter the current.	—||—
Voltmeter	Measures the current.	—(V)—
Ammeter	Measures the voltage.	—(resistor)—

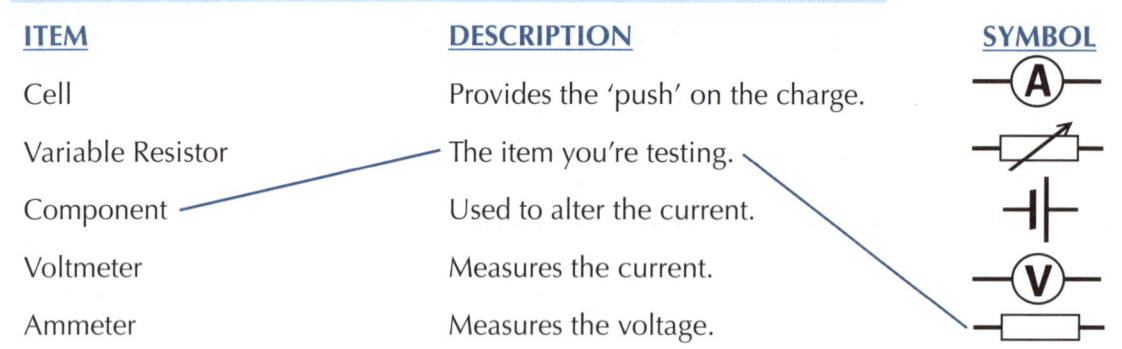

Q2 The diagram below shows a **complete circuit**.

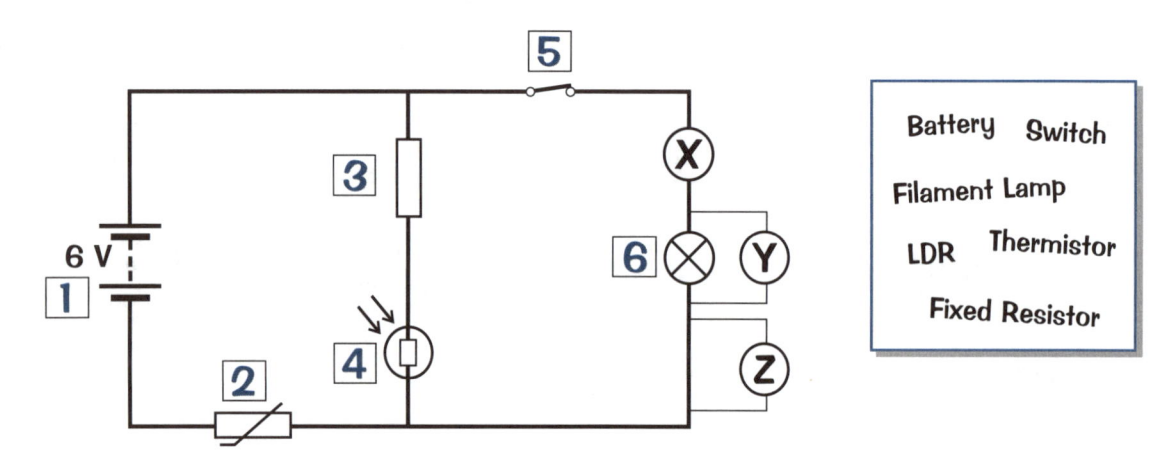

Box: Battery Switch Filament Lamp LDR Thermistor Fixed Resistor

a) Use the words in the box to name each of the numbered components.

1. .... 2. .... 3. ....
4. .... 5. .... 6. ....

b) Components X, Y and Z are voltmeters. Which one is correctly connected to measure the voltage across the lamp? Circle the correct answer.

Voltmeters compare the p.d. between two points.

    X   Y   Z

Q3 Circle the correct word from each pair to complete the following paragraph.

> Voltage (or **P.D.** / **pH**) tells you how much **energy** / **current** is transferred to or from each **resistance** / **charge** as it moves between two points. The battery transfers energy **to** / **from** the charge and components transfer it **to** / **from** the charge. The voltage across a component can be measured by connecting a(n) **voltmeter** / **ammeter** in **series** / **parallel** with it.

Module P5 — Electric Circuits

Resistance

Q1 Tick the boxes to show whether the following statements are **true** or **false**.

		True	False
a)	LDRs and thermistors are types of variable resistor.	☐	☐
b)	An LDR has a high resistance in very bright light.	☐	☐
c)	The resistance of a thermistor increases as the temperature decreases.	☐	☐
d)	An LDR could be part of a useful thermostat.	☐	☐

Q2 Use the equation given to fill in the missing values in the table below.

$$\text{Resistance} = \frac{\text{voltage}}{\text{current}}$$

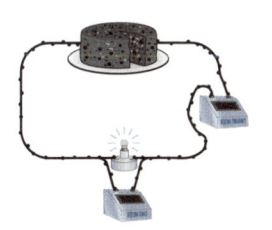

Voltage (V)	Current (A)	Resistance (Ω)
6	2	
8	4	
9	3	
4	8	

Q3 Circle the correct word(s) from each pair to complete the following paragraph.

When **current** / **voltage** flows through a resistor, the temperature of the resistor **decreases** / **increases**. **Filament lamps** / **Motors** make use of this effect. They contain a filament with a very **high** / **low** resistance that gets so **cold** / **hot** when charge passes through it that it **reflects** / **gives out** light.

Q4 Peter's teacher has given him an unlabelled **resistor**. Peter plans an experiment to **work out** its **resistance** but he is worried that the resistance of the **wires** in his test circuit will affect his results.

Tick the boxes to show whether the following statements are **true** or **false**.

		True	False
a)	Connecting wires have no resistance so they won't affect Peter's results.	☐	☐
b)	The resistance of connecting wires is so small that it can usually be ignored.	☐	☐
c)	Peter could work out the resistance by taking pairs of voltage-current readings.	☐	☐
d)	Peter could measure the current flowing in the circuit using a thermistor.	☐	☐

Module P5 — Electric Circuits

Resistance

Q5 The graph shows a **V-I curve** for a component in a circuit.

a) i) Is the component's resistance constant or changing? Circle the correct answer.

      constant   changing

ii) Give a reason for your answer to part i).

....

....

b) i) What current flows through the component when the voltage across it is 2 V?

....

ii) Use your answer to part i) to calculate the component's resistance.

....

c) Sketch a graph on the axes above to show how current varies with voltage for a fixed value resistor with a **higher** resistance than the component shown.

Remember, resistance = voltage ÷ current

Q6 Miriam is testing **two unknown components**, A and B, using a standard test circuit.

a) While Miriam was testing component A, her friend opened the blinds covering the windows. The bright light entering the room changed the resistance of component A.

Circle the correct word from each pair to complete the following sentences about component A.

i) Component A is an **LED** / **LDR**.

ii) Its resistance **increases** / **decreases** when the light intensity increases.

b) Component B is used as part of a thermostat and its resistance changes according to the temperature.

i) What is component B? ....

ii) Describe how the resistance of component B will change as it is gradually warmed.

....

....

LEDr — Light-emitting doctor

Top Tips: There are two very important skills you need to master for resistance questions — **drawing and interpreting V-I graphs** and using the formula **R = V ÷ I**. Make sure you can do both.

Module P5 — Electric Circuits

Series Circuits

Q1 Match up these **descriptions** with what they describe in a **series circuit**.

Same everywhere in the circuit — Potential difference

Shared out between the components — Current

The sum of the resistances — Total potential difference

Can be different for each component — Total resistance

Q2 The diagram shows a series circuit.

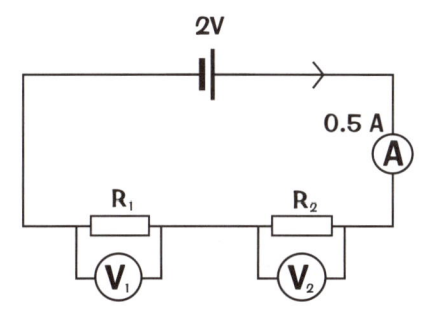

a) What component could be added to the circuit to **increase** the voltage and current? Circle the correct answer.

LDR   cell   voltmeter   ammeter

b) Voltmeter V_1 has a lower reading than voltmeter V_2. Which resistor has the **higher** resistance? Circle the correct answer.

resistor R_1 resistor R_2

c) i) Is the total resistance of the circuit larger or smaller than the resistance of resistor R_1? Circle the correct answer.

larger   smaller

ii) Give a reason for your answer to part i).

....

Q3 Vikram does an experiment with different numbers of identical **lamps** in two **series circuits**. The diagram on the right shows his two circuits.

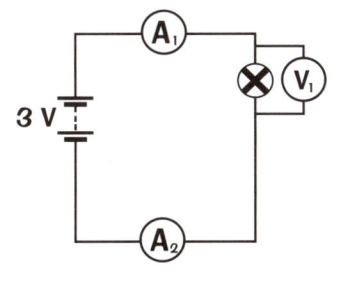

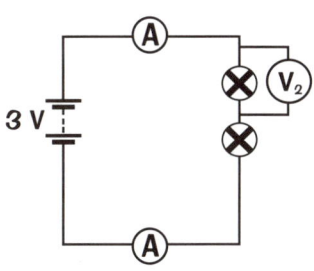

Circle the correct word(s) from each pair to complete the following sentences about the circuits.

a) Ammeters A_1 and A_2 will show **the same / different** readings.

b) Voltmeters V_1 and V_2 will show **the same / different** readings.

c) The total resistance of the circuit with one lamp will be **larger / smaller** than the total resistance of the circuit with two lamps.

Module P5 — Electric Circuits

Parallel Circuits

Q1 Tick the boxes to show whether these statements about parallel circuits are **true** or **false**.

	True	False
a) Each branch of the circuit is connected separately to the power supply.	☐	☐
b) One component can be switched off without affecting the others.	☐	☐
c) The component with the least resistance has the smallest current flowing through it.	☐	☐

Q2 Karen does an experiment with different numbers of identical **lamps** in three **parallel circuits**. The diagrams below show her three circuits.

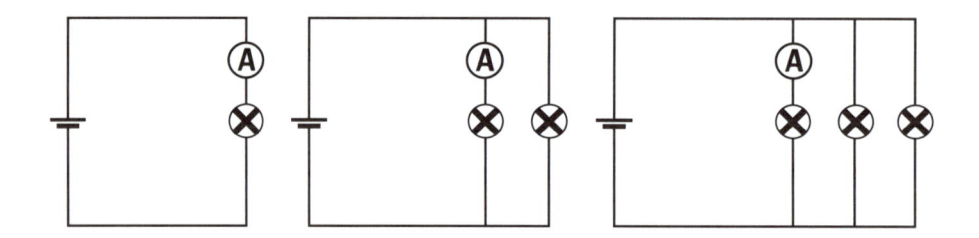

Circle the correct word(s) from each pair to complete the following sentences.

a) The reading on the ammeter **increases / stays the same** as more lamps are added to the circuit because the **current / voltage** through each lamp depends on its **voltage / resistance**.

b) The total current in the circuit **increases / decreases** as more lamps are added because it depends on the total **resistance / voltage** of the circuit.

c) The total resistance of the circuit **increases / decreases** as lamps are added because there are **more / fewer** branches for the charges to flow along.

d) The resistance of each lamp **increases / stays the same** as lamps are added because it depends on the properties of the **lamp / wire**.

Q3 In the circuit below, ammeter A_2 reads **0.27 A** and ammeter A_3 reads **0.43 A**.

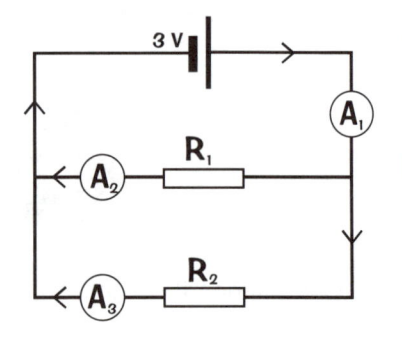

a) Which of the following is the correct way to work out the reading on ammeter A_1? Circle the correct answer.

$$0.27 + 0.43 = 0.7 \text{ A} \qquad 0.43 - 0.27 = 0.16 \text{ A}$$

b) Which resistor has the larger resistance, R_1 or R_2? Give a reason for your answer.

....

....

Module P5 — Electric Circuits

Mains Electricity

Q1 **Mains electricity** is distributed around the country through the **National Grid**.

    a) At what voltage is mains electricity supplied to people's homes?

    ....

    b) How is the current from the mains different from the current supplied by batteries?

    ....

Q2 Inga is experimenting with a **magnet** and a **coil of wire**. She moves the north pole of the magnet **into** the coil and a **positive** voltage is induced.

Circle the correct answers to the following questions.

    a) In which direction will the induced voltage be if Inga:

        i) Moves the magnet back out of the coil?   positive   negative

        ii) Reverses the magnet's north-south polarity, then moves it into the coil in the same way as before?   positive   negative

    b) What voltage will Inga generate if she:

        i) Holds the magnet still inside the coil?

        positive   negative   alternating   none

        ii) Sets up her apparatus so that the magnet moves repeatedly into and out of the coil?

        positive   negative   alternating   none

Q3 Use words from the box to fill in the blanks in this paragraph about generating electricity.

> moving   electromagnetic   magnet   coil   induction
> alternating   voltage   reverses   magnetic

You can create a .... across an electrical conductor by .... a magnet near the conductor. This is called .... In simple generators this is usually done by rotating a .... near a .... of wire. The generator produces a(n) .... current.

Module P5 — Electric Circuits

Mains Electricity

Q4 Look at the simple **generators** sketched below.

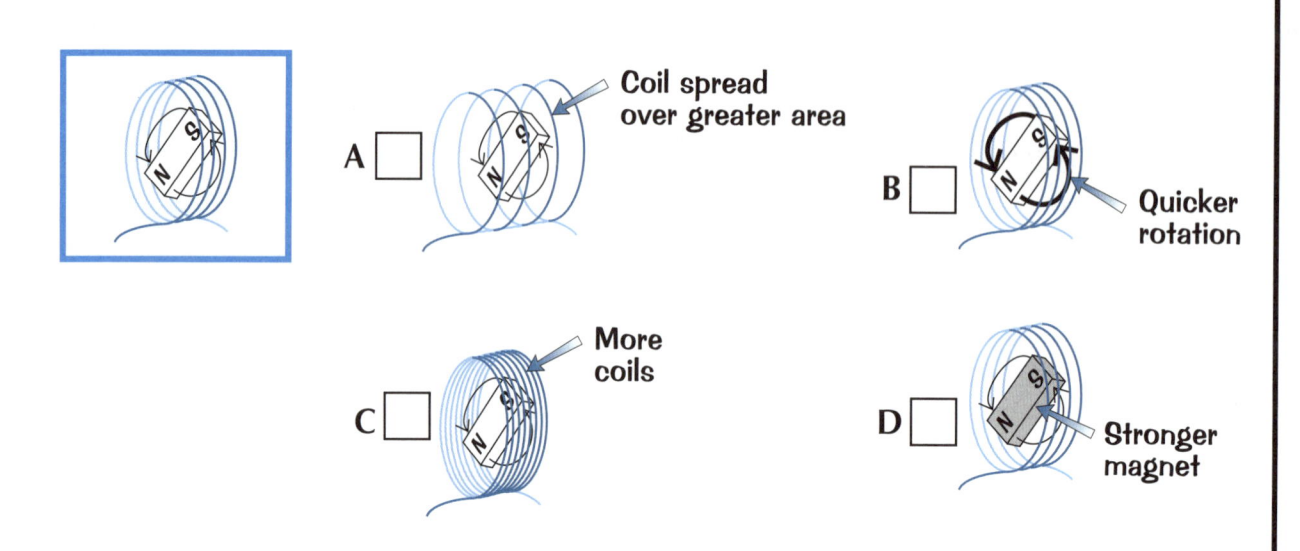

- A: Coil spread over greater area
- B: Quicker rotation
- C: More coils
- D: Stronger magnet

a) Which **one** of the generators labelled A – D will **not** induce a higher voltage than the generator in the blue box? Tick the appropriate box.

b) Give one other way **not** shown in the sketches to increase the voltage induced.

....

Q5 The diagram shows a **hamster-powered generator**.

a) As the hamster tires he begins to run more slowly. How will this affect the voltage generated?

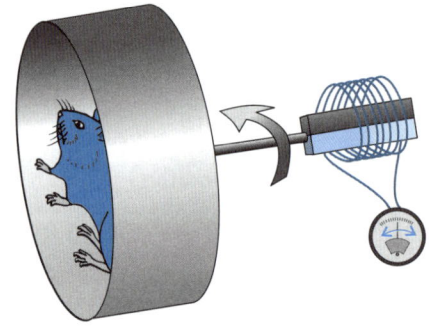

....

....

b) Meg wants to use the generator to charge her mobile phone. The phone needs a 12 V electrical supply but the hamster can only generate a maximum of 2 V. What device could Meg use to increase the voltage to the level needed?

....

c) Will it matter to Meg if the hamster runs in the opposite direction? If so, how? Explain your answer.

....

....

Top Tips: Electromagnetic induction is a very **useful** bit of Physics, because it's how we make all our electricity. The massive generators in a power station work like this — there's a **conductor** experiencing a **changing magnetic field**, and the result is an **induced voltage**.

Module P5 — Electric Circuits

Mains Electricity

Q6 Number the following statements in the right order to explain how a transformer works.

| 1 | An alternating voltage is connected to the primary coil of a transformer. |

| ☐ | This causes a rapidly changing magnetic field in the core. |

| ☐ | An alternating current can flow in a circuit connected to the secondary coil. |

| ☐ | An alternating current flows in the primary coil. |

| ☐ | The changing magnetic field induces an alternating voltage in the secondary coil. |

Q7 Transformers have a **laminated iron core**.

a) Describe the structure of a transformer.

....

....

b) What is the difference between a step-up and a step-down transformer, in terms of:

i) the number of turns on each coil?

....

ii) what they are used for?

....

c) Transformers only work with alternating current. They **won't work** with **direct current**. Explain why.

....

....

....

Module P5 — Electric Circuits

Electrical Energy

Q1 Circle the correct word from each pair to complete the following definition of **electrical power**.

> When electric charge flows through an appliance **energy** / mass is transferred **to** / from the appliance. The power of an appliance is the rate at which it transfers **energy** / mass from the photons / **charge** passing through it.

Q2 The **energy transferred** by an electrical appliance depends on its **power** and the **time** it's on for.

a) Complete the equation relating energy transferred, power and time:

Energy = ... × ....

Watch out for the units here — a watt is a joule per second.

b) Use your answer to part a) to work out the energy transferred by:

   i) a 100 watt lamp in 10 seconds: ....

   ii) a 500 watt motor in 2 minutes: ....

   iii) a 1 kW heater in 20 seconds: ....

Q3 Simon and Polly are discussing the units of **energy** and **power**.

Simon says, "Energy is measured in kilowatt-hours — just like on an electricity bill."
Polly says, "That's wrong, energy is always measured in joules — kilowatt-hours measure power."

a) Who is right? ....

b) Why are there two units for electrical energy?

....

Q4 Lucy is comparing **three lamps**. She connects each lamp in a circuit and measures the **current**. Her results are shown in the table below.

Complete the table by filling in the missing values.

	Lamp A	Lamp B	Lamp C
Voltage (V)	12	3	230
Current (A)	2.5	4	0.1
Power (W)			
Energy used in one minute (J)			

Module P5 — Electric Circuits

Electrical Energy

Q5 Joanna is going to sell **tea and cakes** after a school concert to raise money for charity. She has found the **cost** of all the **ingredients**, but now needs to calculate the **electricity** costs so she can work out how much to charge people.

a) The water boiler in the school canteen has a power rating of 150 W. Joanna estimates they will need to keep it on for half an hour. How much energy will be transferred in this time?

....

Don't forget to use the right units.

b) The school oven has a power of 2.7 kW and will be on for 1 hour and 15 minutes to bake the cakes. How much energy will be transferred in this time?

....

c) The electricity company charges 8.5p per kilowatt-hour.

  i) How much electrical energy will Joanna use in total? ....

  ii) How much will this cost? ....

Q6 Here is an **energy flow diagram** for an electric lamp. Complete the following sentences.

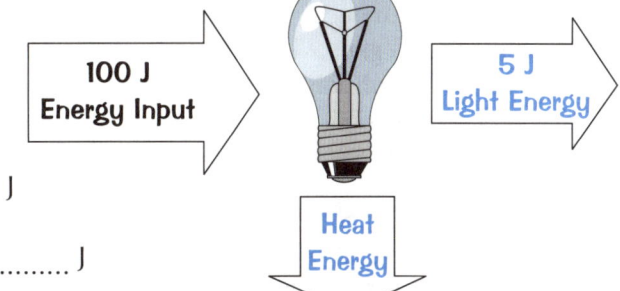

100 J Energy Input → [lamp] → 5 J Light Energy

↓ Heat Energy

a) The **total energy supplied** is .... J

b) The **energy usefully transferred** is .... J

c) The amount of energy **wasted** is .... J

d) The **efficiency** of the lamp is .... %

$$\text{Efficiency} = \frac{\text{energy usefully transferred}}{\text{total energy supplied}} \times 100\%$$

Q7 Use the **efficiency formula** to complete the table.

Total Energy Supplied (J)	Energy Usefully Transferred (J)	Efficiency (%)
2000	1500	
4000	2000	
4000	1000	
600	200	

Top Tips: There are three different equations on these last two pages — make sure you don't get all muddled. The units can be tricky too. P = V × I isn't too bad — it's just watts = volts × amps. But E = P × t could be 'joules = watts × seconds' **OR** 'kWh = kW × h. Hmm. Best to practise now.

Module P5 — Electric Circuits

The National Grid

Q1 Read the passage below and answer the questions that follow.

National Grid Celebrates 75th Birthday

2008 marks the 75th year since the National Grid began operation. The National Grid is the network of cables and pylons that distributes electricity throughout the UK. The idea of a national grid was proposed by Lord Weir in 1925, as a solution to the inefficient and fragmented electricity supply system in operation at that time.

In the early 20th century most of the demand for electricity was for lighting in the homes of the few who could afford it. However, with developments in the technology used to generate AC electricity, large power stations began to be built. This decreased the cost of electricity, meaning that it was affordable for more people to use at home and cost-effective for industry.

As more and more people started to use electricity, problems began to occur. The supply systems often struggled to meet demand — supply would stop altogether or become patchy and unreliable. Another problem was that different power stations supplied electricity at different voltages, which meant that people could only use certain lamps and appliances.

The solution to these problems was the National Grid, which began operating in 1933 as a set of local grids. In 1938 these grids were connected to form the single system we know today. Construction of the National Grid had an enormous impact on the number of houses with an electricity supply — 65% of all houses in the UK were connected by 1938. By 1948, 85% of houses were connected and electricity was no longer the luxury it had once been.

The National Grid revolutionised electricity distribution in the UK, and 75 years on is still going strong. However, it's not particularly efficient (wasting around 30 000 GWh* every year) and the high-voltage power cables across the country can be dangerous and have even been linked with leukaemia.

The method used to maximise the efficiency of the system is to use transformers to distribute electricity with a high voltage (400 000 V) and low current. This allows high power to be transmitted and minimises the heating effect caused by the flow of current, reducing the energy wasted as heat.

As a country, we rely on the National Grid so much that it is difficult to imagine a future without it in one form or another. Scientists are currently researching alternative methods of transmission, including beaming energy from solar power satellites or using superconducting resistance-free cables to end power losses and improve the Grid.

* 1 GWh = 1 000 000 kWh

Module P5 — Electric Circuits

The National Grid

a) Suggest **one** way in which the development of the National Grid benefited society.

....

....

b) In the late 19th century, DC was safer than AC and could be stored. This meant DC was more popular. Which is used in the National Grid today — DC or AC?

....

c) A power station generates electricity at 25 000 V and transmits it at 400 000 V.

   i) What sort of transformer is needed to change the voltage before it is transmitted? Circle the correct answer.

   step-up transformer   **step-down transformer**

   ii) Match the labels below to the correct part of the transformer in the diagram.

   iron core   **magnetic field**   **primary coil**   **secondary coil**

d) The National Grid supplies approximately 370 000 GWh of energy a year to homes and industry. However, as shown in the article, it also wastes 30 000 GWh every year.

   i) Calculate the total energy supplied to the National Grid from power stations.

   ....

   ii) Calculate the efficiency of the National Grid.

   ....

e) Circle the correct word from each pair in the following paragraph to explain why superconducting resistance-free cables would minimise power lost from the cables in the National Grid.

   When current flows through cables with **resistance** / **voltage**, the cables heat up. This heating effect **creates** / **wastes** power. However, in cables without **insulation** / **resistance**, power would not be wasted in this way.

Module P5 — Electric Circuits

Module B6 — Brain and Mind

The Nervous System

Q1 Complete the following passage using words from the box.

> environment   favourable   change   mate
> stimulus   respond   temperature   danger

A .... is any .... in the ....
of an organism, for example a change in air .... It's important
that organisms .... to stimuli to keep themselves in
.... conditions, for example to avoid ....
or when finding a ....

Q2 The **CNS** makes up part of the **nervous system**.

a) What do the letters **CNS** stand for?

....

b) What is the function of the CNS?

....

c) On the diagram label the parts that make up the CNS.

d) The **peripheral nervous system** also plays an important role in the body.

i) Circle the correct word(s) in each pair to complete the following sentence.

> The peripheral nervous system connects the
> eyes / CNS to the rest of the body / feet.

ii) What two components make up the peripheral nervous system?

1. ....

2. ....

e) What type of neurones:

i) carry information **to** the CNS? ....

ii) carry instructions **from** the CNS? ....

Top Tips: It's important that you don't get the **basics** muddled up. There are only **two** bits that make up the **CNS**, everything else is the peripheral nervous system. Also make sure you know the difference between **sensory** and **motor neurones**, otherwise you'll find other bits quite tricky.

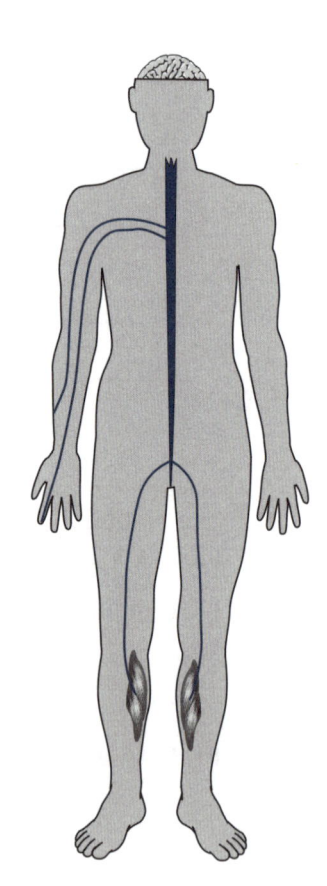

The Nervous System

Q3 Receptors and effectors are important cells in the nervous system.

a) Draw lines to match up the type of cells with their function(s).

receptors

effectors

bring about a change

detect stimuli

respond to nerve impulses

b) Put the words below into the correct columns in the table to show the different types of effectors and receptors, and the different **organs** they form part of.

sound receptor cells   ~~taste buds~~   glands   the eye   muscle cells

the ear   hormone secreting cells   ~~the tongue~~   muscles   light receptor cells

	Example	Make up part of...
Receptor	taste buds	the tongue
Effector		

Q4 Jamie was cooking his mum some tea when he accidentally picked up a **hot** saucepan. Jamie **instantly** dropped the pan back onto the hob.

Put numbers in the boxes so that the following statements are in the correct order to describe how Jamie's nervous system responded to him picking up the hot pan. The first one has been done for you.

☐ Some of the muscles in Jamie's hand contract, causing him to drop the pan.

[1] Temperature receptors in Jamie's hand detect the increase in temperature.

☐ Impulses travel along a motor neurone.

☐ Impulses travel along a sensory neurone.

☐ The information is processed by the spinal cord.

Module B6 — Brain and Mind

The Nervous System

Q5 Complete the diagram using the words provided to show the route of an impulse through the **nervous system**.

sensory neurone   CNS   receptor   effector   motor neurone

Stimulus → ☐ → ☐ → ☐ → ☐ → ☐ → Response

Q6 The diagram below shows a typical **neurone**.

(Diagram labelled: Nucleus, Cell body, Y, X)

a) How does information travel along the neurone?

....

b) Complete the following sentences by circling the correct word in each pair.

> Structure X is the **synapse** / **axon** of the neurone. It's made from the neurone's **cytoplasm** / **nucleus** stretched into a long fibre and surrounded by a cell **membrane** / **wall**.

c) i) Name the part labelled **Y**.

....

ii) What is the **function** of part Y? Tick the correct box(es).

- To keep the neurone warm. ☐
- To increase the speed of transmission of a nerve impulse. ☐
- To slow down the speed of transmission of a nerve impulse. ☐
- To insulate the neurone from neighbouring cells. ☐

d) The neurones in the body aren't directly connected together — there are small **gaps** between them.

i) What name is given to the small gap between neurones?

....

ii) Name two types of chemical that can affect the transmission of impulses across this gap.

1. .... 2. ....

Module B6 — Brain and Mind

Reflexes

Q1 Circle the correct word(s) in each pair to complete the following sentences.

a) Reflexes happen more **quickly** / slowly than considered responses.

b) The neurones involved in reflexes go through the back bone / **spinal cord** or **an unconscious** / a conscious part of the brain.

c) Reflexes are voluntary / **involuntary**.

d) The main purpose of a reflex is to **protect** / display an organism.

e) The nervous pathway of a reflex is called a reflex **arc** / ellipse.

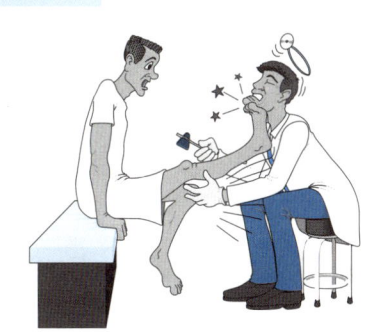

Q2 When you touch something hot with a finger you **automatically** pull the finger away. This is an example of a reflex action.

a) Complete the passage using words from the box below.

| motor   sensory   receptors   effector   relay   stimulus   CNS |

When the .... is detected by .... in the finger an impulse is sent along a .... neurone to the .... The impulse is then passed to a .... neurone. The impulse is relayed to a .... neurone, which carries the impulse to the ....

b) The diagram opposite shows some parts of the nervous system involved in a reflex action. Write the letter that shows:

i) a relay neurone ....

ii) a motor neurone ....

iii) a sensory neurone ....

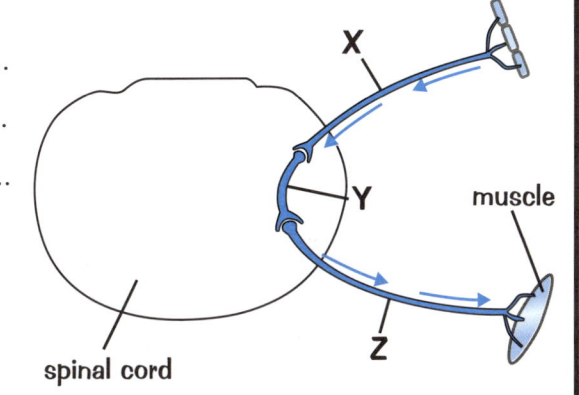

Top Tips: Reflexes are really fast — that's the whole point of them. And the fewer synapses the signals have to cross, the faster the reaction. Doctors test people's reflexes by tapping below their knees to make their legs jerk. This reflex takes less than 50 milliseconds as only two synapse are involved.

Module B6 — Brain and Mind

Reflexes

Q3 **Earthworms** rely on **reflexes** for most of their behaviour.
Tick the correct box below to give one **disadvantage** of this.

They cannot respond quickly enough to stimuli. ☐

They have difficulty responding to new situations. ☐

They'll never be able to learn how to knit. ☐

Q4 Draw lines to match the reflex with the way in which it **helps** the animal **survive**.

- a bird making its feathers stand on end
- a turtle retracting its head and limbs into its shell
- a jellyfish moving its tentacles when it senses movement
- a spider running onto its web when it feels it move
- a mollusc closing its shell

- finding food
- sheltering from a predator
- finding a mate

Q5 Look carefully at the diagrams showing two different **eyes** below.

Eye A   Eye B (pupil labelled)

a) Which diagram do you think shows an eye in **bright light**? Give a reason for your answer.

....

....

b) Complete the following passage using words from the box below.

| considered | quickly | reflex | slowly | adjust | damaged |

The eye's response to light is a .... response, these responses happen

very .... This helps your eyes .... quickly to dim

light, and stops them being .... by sudden bright lights.

Module B6 — Brain and Mind

Brain Development and Learning

Q1 Tick the boxes to show whether each statement is **true** or **false**.

    True   False

a) The brain contains around one million neurones. ☐ ☐

b) Complex animals with a brain are able to learn by experience. ☐ ☐

c) The brain coordinates complex behaviour such as social behaviour. ☐ ☐

Q2 Complete the two passages using words from the box below to explain how the **environment** can affect brain **development**.

> more   trillions   unconnected   formed
> experience   network   less   developed   stimulated

Most of the neurone connections in a newborn baby's brain are not yet ...., so the brain is only partly ....

Every new .... causes the brain to become .... developed.

When neurones in the brain are .... they branch out, forming connections between cells that were previously ....

This forms a massive .... of neurones with .... of different pathways for impulses to travel down.

Q3 Why are **complex animals**, such as humans, able to **adapt** to new situations better than **simple animals**, such as insects? Circle the correct answer.

- Simple animals have slower brains.
- Complex organisms have a larger variety of potential pathways in their brains.
- The pathways in the brains of complex organisms are thicker.

Top Tips: Brain development is a really tricky subject — I always think of it as kind of like exploring a jungle. There are loads of paths through the jungle and as people explore more of the environment they form new connections (paths) linking the paths that were already there.

Module B6 — Brain and Mind

Brain Development and Learning

Q4 Sarah and Sophie both play the piano. Sarah has been **practising all week** but Sophie **hasn't practised at all**. The girls' piano teacher, Mr Fudge, compliments Sarah on her performance but tells Sophie that she needs to practise more next week.

Complete the passage using words from the box below to explain why Sarah was so much better than Sophie.

| strengthened | pathways | transmit | repeated |

When experiences are .... over and over again the .... that they travel down become .... These pathways are more likely to .... nerve impulses than others.

Q5 Hew has been in a **car accident**. Bruising on his head suggests that he took a nasty blow during the crash. The doctors are also concerned that he may have **damaged** an area of his **brain** because he's having difficulty speaking and is unable to remember simple facts.

a) i) What part of Hew's **brain** might have been **damaged**?

....

ii) On the diagram below, label the part that you named in part i).

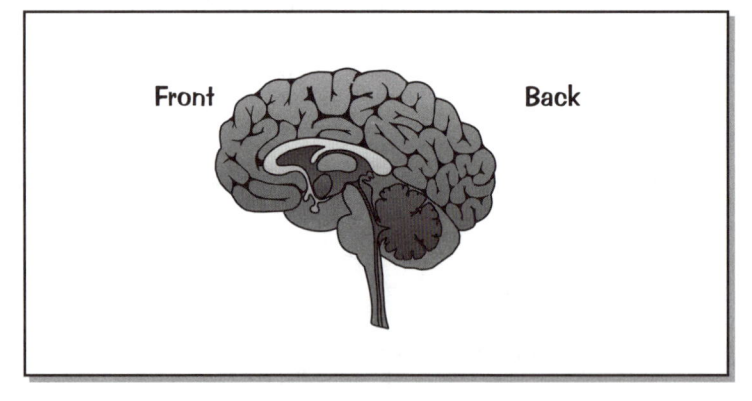

b) The damaged part of Hew's brain is involved in language and memory. Name **two** other things that this part of the brain is important for.

1. ....

2. ....

Top Tips: Learning is a really tricky subject, even the best scientists aren't sure exactly how it all works. At least you can use what you've learnt to help with your **revision** — **repeating** things over and over again makes sure they're well and truly lodged in your bonce.

Module B6 — Brain and Mind

Studying the Brain

Q1 Studying the brain can be useful for a number of reasons, for example in the **diagnosis** of people with brain disorders such as Parkinson's disease. Describe how the following methods used by scientists to **map** the regions of the **cortex**.

a) Studying patients with brain damage ....

....

b) Electrically stimulating the brain ....

....

c) MRI scans ....

....

Q2 There are two main types of **memory** — **short-term** and **long-term**.

a) Draw lines to match the types of memory with the correct descriptions.

short-term memory	includes things you're currently thinking about
long-term memory	stored memories from days, weeks, months or years ago
	lasts from a few seconds to a few hours

b) Where are the following memories likely to be stored? Put a letter **S** in the boxes next to any memories likely to be stored in **short-term** memory and a letter **L** in those likely to be stored in **long-term** memory.

- The rides you went on when you visited a theme park last month. ☐
- The smell of hot apple pie drifting through from the kitchen as it's being baked. ☐
- What you had for tea last Wednesday. ☐
- Something that happened in an episode of The Bill half an hour ago. ☐
- What your great aunt Gladys got you for your birthday when you were fourteen. ☐
- Answering a question in an exam about a topic you learnt two months ago. ☐

c) Why is the study of memory an ongoing area of research? Underline the correct answer.

The brain is evolving so rapidly that theories quickly become out of date.

No model has yet been produced that provides an adequate explanation of memory.

Module B6 — Brain and Mind

Memory Mapping

Q1 Read the passage below and answer the questions that follow.

The ability to store information in our brains for retrieval later on is something that most of us take for granted. Certain areas of the brain are crucial for memory processing — the discovery of some of these areas has come from attempts to treat people with epilepsy.

Epilepsy is a condition that causes sufferers to have repeated seizures. The cause of a seizure is not usually known, but they are always accompanied by a change in the electrical activity in the cerebral cortex of the brain. The abnormal electrical activity tends to start in an area where the neurones are highly sensitive, and then spread out across the cortex. Epileptic seizures can often be controlled using anticonvulsant drugs, and sometimes with surgery.

Between the 1930s and 1950s, Wilder Penfield investigated the areas of his patients' brains that were prone to seizures using electrical stimulation. By systematically stimulating points in the cortex, Penfield was able to determine the link between certain areas and their functions. For example, when he stimulated a particular area patients would feel tingling sensations in their skin, showing that this area was involved in the sense of touch. When he stimulated a region of the brain called the temporal lobe (shown in the diagram) some of his patients seemed to experience memories of past events — suggesting that the temporal lobe is part of the system for recalling stored memories.

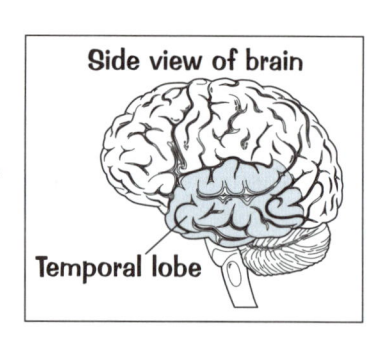

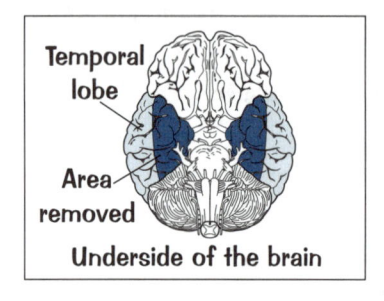

Further evidence for the involvement of the temporal lobe in memory came from a patient who was given surgery for his epilepsy in 1953. The patient, known as H.M., had part of the temporal lobe on both sides of his brain removed to try to control his seizures. The diagram shows the areas removed.

The operation was successful, in that H.M.'s seizures were reduced, but it left him with severe amnesia (memory loss). The interesting thing about H.M.'s amnesia was that it was very selective. H.M. can remember the experiences of his childhood, showing that his long-term memories stored before the operation were not affected. He is also able to learn new tasks and retain details of what he is doing, showing that his short-term memory still works. However, what H.M. can't do is form any new long-term memories. For example, the doctor who has worked with H.M. for over 40 years since the operation has to reintroduce herself every time they meet — H.M. has no memory of who she is.

Since the case of H.M. doctors have investigated other ways to map the areas of a patient's brain involved in memory. One method currently used is to take MRI scans of a patient's brain while they are performing memory tasks. MRI scans use a strong magnetic field to monitor changes in the blood flow around the brain and highlight areas of high activity. The theory is that by working out the areas that are active during the memory tasks, the scientist can determine which areas are needed for memory processing.

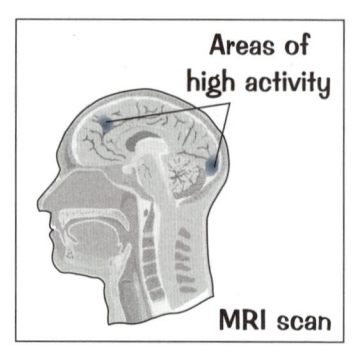

It is hoped that in the future a model will be devised that fully explains how our brains process memories — until then it remains an ongoing area of research.

Module B6 — Brain and Mind

Memory Mapping

a) Complete the definition of memory by filling in the blanks.

> Memory is the .... and .... of information.

b) Give three methods mentioned in the article that have been used by scientists to map the cortex.

1. ....
2. ....
3. ....

c) What type of memory was recalled when Penfield stimulated the temporal lobe? Circle the correct answer.

long-term memory   short-term memory   mid-term memory

d) Which area of the brain is responsible for recalling past memories?

....

e) Tick the box(es) to show which parts of H.M.'s memory were:

  i) Unaffected by his operation.

  All long-term memories. ☐
  Short-term memories. ☐
  The ability to recall long-term memories. ☐
  The ability to form new long-term memories. ☐

  ii) Damaged by his operation.

  All long-term memories. ☐
  Short-term memories. ☐
  The ability to recall long-term memories. ☐
  The ability to form new long-term memories. ☐

f) Which sentence in the article suggests that there isn't yet a model that provides an adequate explanation for memory.

....

....

....

H.M.'s memory is an ongoing area of research, and an important tourist attraction.

Module B6 — Brain and Mind

Module C6 — Chemical Synthesis

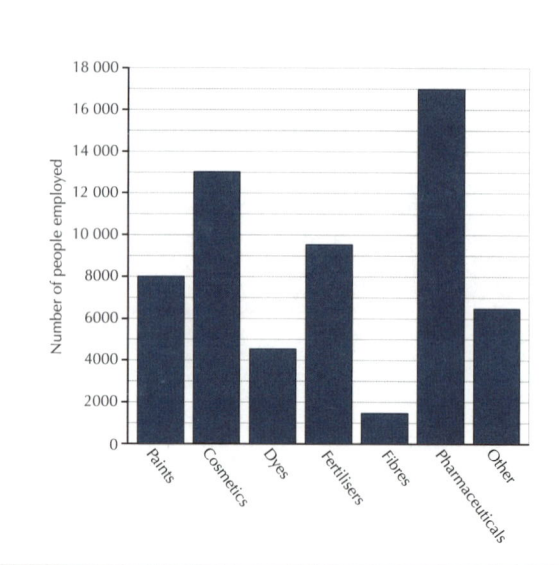

Industrial Chemical Synthesis

Q1 Complete the following sentence by circling the correct word(s) in each pair.

> Chemical synthesis is the manufacture of **simple / complex** chemical compounds from **simpler / more complex** ones.

Q2 Tick the boxes to show whether the following are usually produced on a **small** or **large scale**.

	Small scale	Large scale
a) Pharmaceuticals	☐	☐
b) Sulfuric acid	☐	☐

Q3 Modern industry uses thousands of tonnes of **sulfuric acid** per day. The pie chart shows the major **uses** of the sulfuric acid produced by a particular plant.

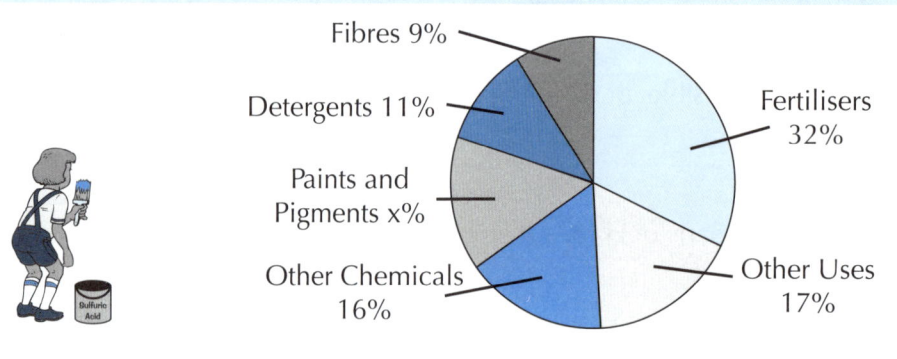

Pie chart values:
- Fibres 9%
- Detergents 11%
- Paints and Pigments x%
- Other Chemicals 16%
- Fertilisers 32%
- Other Uses 17%

a) What is the **main use** of the sulfuric acid from this plant?

....

b) What percentage of the sulfuric acid from this plant is used in the production of paints and pigments?

....

Q4 The bar chart shows the number of people **employed** in various sectors of the **chemical industry** in country X.

a) Which **sector** employs the **most** people?

....

b) Approximately how many people **in total** are employed in the chemical industry in country X? Circle the correct answer.

    50 000   60 000   80 000

Acids and Alkalis

Q1 Complete each of the following sentences with a single word.

a) Solutions which are not acidic or alkaline are said to be ....

b) A neutral substance has a pH of ....

c) Universal indicator is a combination of different ....

d) An alkali is a substance with a pH .... than 7.

Q2 Draw lines to match the substances and their universal indicator colours to their **pH** values and **acid/alkali strengths**.

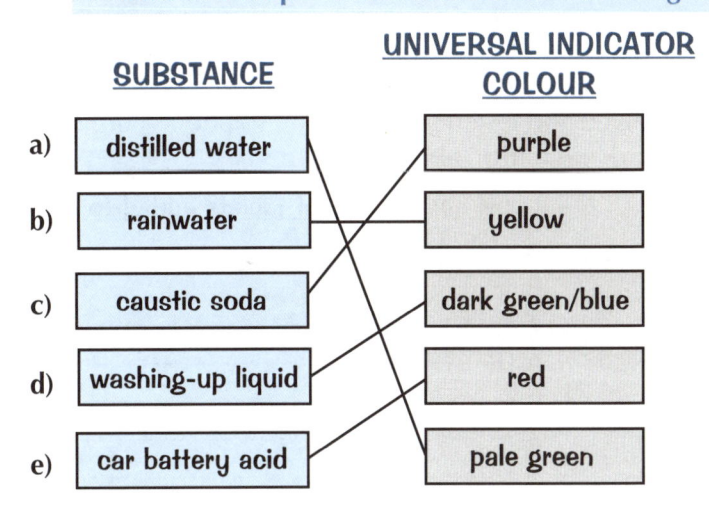

SUBSTANCE	UNIVERSAL INDICATOR COLOUR	pH	ACID/ALKALI STRENGTH
a) distilled water	purple	5/6	strong alkali
b) rainwater	yellow	8/9	weak alkali
c) caustic soda	dark green/blue	14	weak acid
d) washing-up liquid	red	7	neutral
e) car battery acid	pale green	1	strong acid

Q3 Many chemicals that people use **every day** are **acids** or **alkalis**.

a) Complete the following passage using words from the box.

| hydrogen chloride | solids | more | tartaric | ethanoic | less | liquid | nitric |

Acids are substances with a pH of .... than 7.

Pure acidic compounds are found in various different states, for example citric acid and .... acid are both ....

Sulfuric acid is an example of a .... acidic compound, as are .... and .... acids.

There are also acidic compounds that are gases — .... is one example.

b) Name three common **alkalis** that are **hydroxides**.

....

Module C6 — Chemical Synthesis

Acids and Alkalis

Q4 **Indigestion** is caused by **too much acid** in the stomach.
Antacid tablets contain **alkalis**, which neutralise the excess acid.

a) Which is the correct word equation for a **neutralisation reaction**? Circle the correct answer.

salt + acid → alkali + water   acid + alkali → salt + water   acid + water → alkali + salt

b) Say what ions are produced when:

i) an acidic compound is dissolved in water.

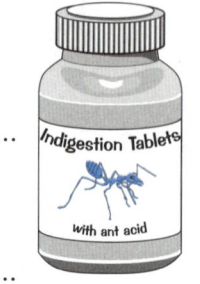

....

ii) an alkaline compound is dissolved in water.

....

Joey wanted to test whether some antacid tablets really did **neutralise acid**. He added a tablet to some hydrochloric acid, stirred it until it dissolved and tested the pH of the solution. Further tests were carried out after dissolving a second, third and fourth tablet.
His results are shown in the table below.

Tablets added	pH of acid
0	1
1	2
2	3
3	7
4	7

pH against no. of tablets added to acid

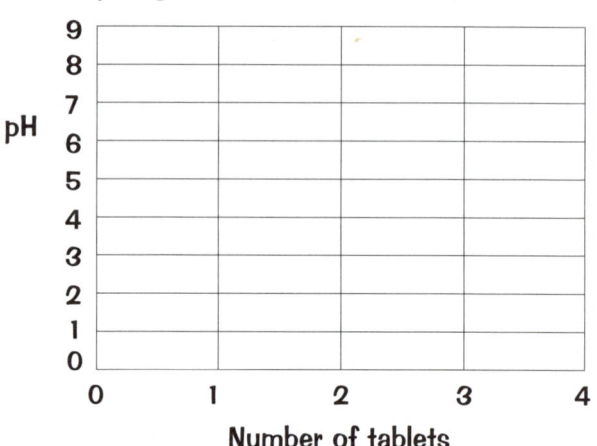

c) i) Plot a graph of the results on the grid shown.

ii) How many tablets were needed to neutralise the acid? ....

d) Give two ways Joey could have tested the pH of the solution.

1. ....

2. ....

Q5 When an acid and an alkali react the products are **neutral**. This is called a **neutralisation** reaction.

a) Describe what happens to the **hydrogen ions** from the acid and the **hydroxide ions** from the alkali during a neutralisation reaction.

....

b) Write a symbol equation to illustrate the reaction between the **hydrogen ions** from the acid and the **hydroxide ions** from the alkali during a neutralisation reaction.

....

Module C6 — Chemical Synthesis

Acids Reacting with Metals

Q1 Shirley is observing the reactions between various acids and metals.

a) Describe what you would expect to observe when aluminium reacts with dilute hydrochloric acid.

....

....

b) Complete the word equation for the general reaction between a metal and an acid.

ACID + METAL → .... + ...

Q2 Tick the boxes to show whether the following statements are **true** or **false**.

		True	False
a)	All metals react with acids.	☐	☐
b)	Sulfates are always formed when sulfuric acid reacts with a metal.	☐	☐
c)	Hydrochloric acid produces hydrate salts.	☐	☐
d)	The more reactive a metal the slower it will react with an acid.	☐	☐
e)	The gas produced when a metal reacts with an acid explodes with a squeaky pop.	☐	☐

Q3 The diagram below shows **magnesium** reacting with dilute **hydrochloric acid**.

a) Label the diagram with the names of the chemicals.

b) Complete the word equation for this reaction:

magnesium + ... → magnesium chloride + ...

c) Zinc reacts with sulfuric acid. Give the **word** equation for this reaction.

....

Module C6 — Chemical Synthesis

Oxides, Hydroxides and Carbonates

Q1 One type of neutralisation reaction is the reaction between an acid and a metal oxide.

a) Complete the general equation for the reaction between a metal oxide and an acid.

ACID + METAL OXIDE → .... + ...

b) Which combination of substances would react in this way?
Choose the correct answer from the options below by ticking **one** box.

Magnesium and sulfuric acid. ☐

Sodium hydroxide and water. ☐

Copper oxide and hydrochloric acid. ☐

A metal-ox-hide

Q2 The reactions between acids and metal hydroxides are also neutralisation reactions.

a) Complete the general equation for the reaction between a metal hydroxide and an acid.

ACID + METAL HYDROXIDE → .... + ...

b) The symbol equation below shows the reaction between sulfuric acid solution and sodium hydroxide solution.

$$H_2SO_4(\text{......}) + 2NaOH(\text{......}) \rightarrow Na_2SO_4(\text{......}) + 2H_2O(\text{......})$$

i) Complete the equation by adding the state symbols.

ii) Write out a word equation for this reaction.

....

Q3 Fill in the blanks to complete the word equations for **acids** reacting with **metal oxides** and **metal hydroxides**.

a) hydrochloric acid + lead oxide → .... chloride + water

b) nitric acid + copper hydroxide → copper .... + water

Remember nitric acid produces nitrates.

c) sulfuric acid + zinc oxide → zinc sulfate + ...

d) hydrochloric acid + ... oxide → nickel .... + ...

e) .... acid + copper oxide → .... nitrate + ...

f) sulfuric acid + ... hydroxide → sodium .... + ...

Top Tips: At first glance it looks quite scary, all this writing equations — but it's not that bad, honest. The key is to learn the basic rules inside out. Once you've got them mastered it's really just a case of swapping a few bits round and filling in the gaps. No reason to panic at all.

Module C6 — Chemical Synthesis

Oxides, Hydroxides and Carbonates

Q4 Acids reacting with metal carbonates are other examples of neutralisation reactions.

a) Complete the general equation for the reaction between an acid and a metal carbonate.

ACID + METAL CARBONATE → .... + ... + ...

b) Complete the following word equations for the reactions between acids and metal carbonates.

i) sulfuric acid + copper carbonate → ....

ii) nitric acid + magnesium carbonate → ....

iii) sulfuric acid + lithium carbonate → ....

iv) hydrochloric acid + calcium carbonate → ....

v) sulfuric acid + sodium carbonate → ....

c) The reaction below shows another reaction between an aqueous acid and a solid metal carbonate. Complete the equation by adding state symbols.

$2HCl(\text{......}) + Na_2CO_3(\text{......}) \rightarrow 2NaCl(\text{......}) + H_2O(\text{......}) + CO_2(\text{......})$

Q5 Amir was investigating how he could restore a tarnished copper ornament. He obtained some copper compounds and looked at the effect of reacting them with dilute hydrochloric acid (HCl).

SUBSTANCE TESTED	FORMULA	COLOUR	OBSERVATIONS WHEN ADDED TO THE ACID
copper carbonate	$CuCO_3$	green	fizzed and dissolved forming a blue solution
copper hydroxide	$Cu(OH)_2$	blue	dissolved slowly forming a blue solution
copper oxide	CuO	black	dissolved very slowly forming a blue solution

a) i) Why does copper carbonate fizz when it reacts with an acid?

....

ii) Write a word equation for the reaction between hydrochloric acid and copper carbonate.

....

b) Amir tested part of the copper ornament with the acid and it fizzed. Which compound is likely to be present on the surface of the ornament?

....

Module C6 — Chemical Synthesis

Synthesising Compounds

Q1 Draw lines to match each description to the type of reaction it is describing.

an acid and an alkali react to produce a salt — precipitation

a compound breaks down on heating — neutralisation

an insoluble solid forms when two solutions are mixed — thermal decomposition

Q2 In the synthesis of any **organic chemical** there are a number of **important stages**.

a) Complete the passage using words from the box below.

harmed	reduce	hazards	injury	action

A risk assessment should identify any stage in the process that could cause .... This usually involves identifying .... and the people who might be .... Risk assessments also include what .... can be taken to .... the risk.

b) Give **two** factors that should be considered when choosing the apparatus in which a reaction will be carried out.

....

....

Q3 Explain why each of the following might be carried out during chemical synthesis.

a) Filtration

....

b) Evaporation

....

c) Drying

....

Module C6 — Chemical Synthesis

Synthesising Compounds

Q4 Read the article below and answer the questions that follow.

Sodium Bromide
To most people sodium bromide looks like any other white, crystalline salt. What people don't realise is the vast number of uses it has in the chemical industry, ranging from photography to pharmaceuticals. As with most inorganic chemicals, there are a number of different stages in the production of sodium bromide.

Industrial Synthesis
Sodium bromide (NaBr) is usually produced by reacting sodium hydroxide (NaOH) with hydrobromic acid (HBr):

sodium hydroxide + hydrobromic acid → sodium bromide + water

Although this is a relatively simple reaction, the plant used to produce sodium bromide is quite high-tech. Sodium hydroxide is highly reactive so it's important to use the right equipment. The reaction vessel must be able to withstand the corrosive effects of sodium hydroxide and the large amount of heat produced when it reacts with hydrobromic acid.

The production of sodium bromide doesn't involve a catalyst, so the main way to control the rate of reaction is to alter the concentrations of the reactants.

After reacting sodium hydroxide with hydrobromic acid, the sodium bromide is extracted by evaporation — this involves heating the sodium bromide solution. The water is evaporated, leaving behind white crystals of sodium bromide. After the product has been isolated it is then purified.

Yield and purity
The yield of sodium bromide produced is then calculated. For financial reasons it's important to produce a high yield, so chemical engineers are always looking for ways to modify the process to give a higher yield. The purity of the product is also calculated at this stage.

Safety
People working on sodium bromide production need to take a number of safety precautions. This is because of the highly corrosive and reactive nature of the sodium hydroxide. Sodium bromide also has its risks — it's harmful if swallowed and can irritate the skin and eyes.

Uses of sodium bromide
Sodium bromide has a range of different uses in the chemical industry. The data on the right is from a large chemical company that supplies sodium bromide to different sectors in the chemical industry. It shows what the sodium bromide it produces is used for.

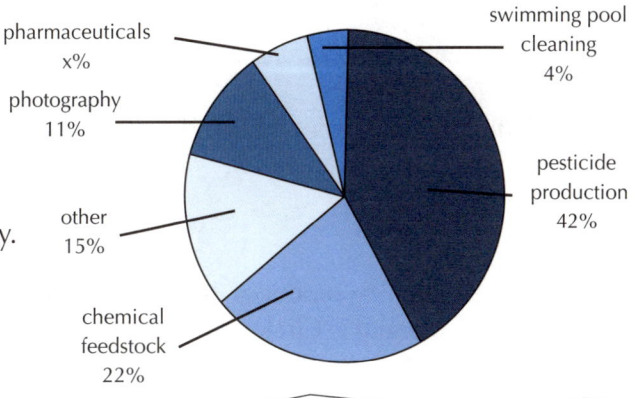

- pharmaceuticals x%
- photography 11%
- other 15%
- chemical feedstock 22%
- swimming pool cleaning 4%
- pesticide production 42%

Module C6 — Chemical Synthesis

Synthesising Compounds

a) What **type** of reaction is used to produce sodium bromide? Circle the correct answer.

    oxidation   esterification   neutralisation   fermentation

b) Give **two** reasons why it is important to choose a suitable reaction vessel for the production of sodium bromide.

   ....

   ....

c) Complete the following sentence by circling the correct word in each pair.

> The sodium bromide is extracted by **evaporation** / **filtration**,
>
> as it is **insoluble** / **soluble** in water.

d) Suggest a method that could be used to **purify** the sodium bromide.

   ....

e) The article describes how sodium hydroxide and sodium bromide are dangerous.

   i) When planning the synthesis of any compound, what is the process of identifying possible hazards called?

   ....

   ii) Give two hazards associated with **sodium bromide**.

   ....

   ....

f) Why is it useful to calculate the **yield** of sodium bromide?

   ....

g) i) Which industry does the company in the article supply the most sodium bromide to?

   ....

   ii) What percentage of their sodium bromide is used in the pharmaceutical industry? Circle the correct answer.

    22%   6%   94%   16%

   iii) If the company produces 3000 tonnes of sodium bromide per year, what mass is used in photography? Circle the correct answer.

    330 tonnes   45 tonnes   450 tonnes   33 tonnes

Module C6 — Chemical Synthesis

Relative Formula Mass

Q1 All elements have a relative atomic mass, A_r.

a) Complete the following sentence by filling in the blanks.

> The relative atomic mass of an element shows the .... of its atoms relative to the mass of one .... of ....

b) Give the **relative atomic masses** (A_r) of the following elements. Use the periodic table to help you.

i) magnesium ....
ii) neon ....
iii) oxygen ....
iv) hydrogen ....
v) C ....
vi) Cu ....
vii) K ....
viii) Ca ....
ix) Cl ....

Q2 Use the periodic table to identify the elements A, B and C.

> Element A has an A_r of 4.
> Element B has an A_r 3 times that of element A.
> Element C has an A_r 4 times that of element A.

A_r me hearties

Element A = ...
Element B = ...
Element C = ...

Q3 a) Explain how the **relative formula mass** of a **compound** is calculated.

....

b) Give the **relative formula masses** (M_r) of the following:

i) water, H_2O ....

ii) potassium chloride, KOH ....

iii) nitric acid, HNO_3 ....

iv) magnesium hydroxide, $Mg(OH)_2$ ....

v) iron(III) hydroxide, $Fe(OH)_3$ ....

Top Tips: The periodic table really comes in useful here. There's no way you'll be able to answer these questions without one (unless you've memorised all the elements' relative atomic masses — and that would just be silly). And luckily for you, you'll be given one in your exam. Yay!

Module C6 — Chemical Synthesis

Isolating the Product and Measuring Yield

Q1 James wanted to produce **silver chloride** (AgCl). He added a carefully measured mass of silver nitrate to some dilute hydrochloric acid. An **insoluble white solid** formed.

a) Complete the formula for calculating percentage yield, and its labels, using words from the box. Words can be used more than once.

| reactants | weighing | theoretical yield | pure | dried | actual yield | maximum |

This is the mass of pure dry product. It is found by ………………………… the dried product.

percentage yield = (………………………… / …………………………) × 100

This is the ………………………… of the product as a percentage of the ………………………… .

This is the ………………………… amount of …………………………, dried product that could have been made using the amounts of ………………………… you started with.

b) James calculated that he should get 2.7 g of silver chloride, but he only got 1.2 g. What was the **percentage yield**?

……

c) What **method** should James use to separate silver chloride from the solution?

……………………………………………………………………………………………

Silver chloride is an insoluble solid.

d) James left the silver chloride to dry on the bench. Suggest two ways the product could have been dried if the reaction was being carried out on a large scale.

1. ………

2. ………

Q2 Emilio and Julio need to separate a **soluble solid** from a **solution**.

a) Which method could they use to separate the solid from solution? Circle the correct answer.

    filtration   evaporation and crystallisation   neutralisation

b) How can the method you suggested in part a) be useful when purifying a product?

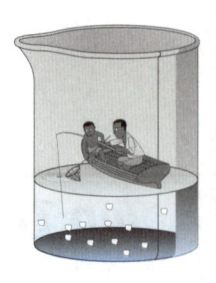

……

Module C6 — Chemical Synthesis

Titrations

Q1 **Titrations** are used widely in industry when determining the **purity** of a substance.

a) If a solid product is being tested why must it first be made into a **solution**?

....

b) Fill in the blanks using words from the box below to describe how a solution is made, and draw lines to connect each statement to the diagram it describes. You can use the words more than once.

| solvent | weigh | swirl | dissolved | crush | water | titration |

① .... the solid product into a powder.

② .... some of the powdered product into a .... flask.

③ The powder is then .... by adding some .... (e.g. ....).

④ .... the flask until all of the solid has ....

c) Label the following pieces of apparatus used in a titration experiment.

....

....

d) Describe how you would carry out a titration.

....

....

....

Module C6 — Chemical Synthesis

Purity

Q1 **Pharmaceutical companies** need to ensure that the drugs they produce are **pure**.

a) Give two methods that can be used to improve the purity of a product.

1. .... 2. ....

b) Circle the correct word in each pair to complete the following sentence explaining why it's important to control the purity of chemicals such as pharmaceuticals.

> Chemicals which are consumed by humans must be **safe** / **insoluble**.
>
> Impurities in drugs could be **illegal** / **dangerous**.

Q2 Ruth works in the quality assurance department of a company that produces **fizzy drinks**. The drinks contain **citric acid**. One of Ruth's jobs is to test the **purity** of the citric acid before it is used to make the drinks. She does this by carrying out an acid-alkali **titration**.

a) What type of reaction do titrations involve? Circle the correct answer.

    precipitation   esterification   neutralisation

b) Ruth starts off with **0.3 g of citric acid** dissolved in **25 cm³** of water. When she carries out the titration she finds that it takes **21.6 cm³ of 2.5 g/dm³ sodium hydroxide** (NaOH) to neutralise the citric acid. Calculate the purity of the citric acid by completing the following steps.

i) Calculate the **concentration** of the citric acid solution using the equation:

$$\text{conc. of citric acid solution} = 4.8 \times \frac{\text{conc. of NaOH} \times \text{vol. of NaOH}}{\text{vol. of citric acid solution}}$$

....

....

ii) Calculate the **mass** of the citric acid using the equation:

$$\text{mass of citric acid} = \text{concentration of citric acid} \times \text{volume}$$

....

iii) Calculate the **percentage purity** of the citric acid using the equation:

$$\% \text{ purity} = \frac{\text{calculated mass of citric acid}}{\text{mass of citric acid at start}} \times 100\%$$

....

....

Module C6 — Chemical Synthesis

Rates of Reaction

Q1 a) Match these common chemical reactions to the **speed** at which they happen.

a firework exploding	SLOW (hours or longer)	a match burning
hair being dyed	MODERATE SPEED (minutes)	a ship rusting
an apple rotting	FAST (seconds or shorter)	

b) Complete the following sentence by circling the correct word in each pair.

The rate of a reaction is how fast **products / reactants** are changed into **products / reactants**.

Q2 When chemicals are produced on an **industrial scale** it is important to control the **rates of reactions**.

Complete the passage below using words from the box.

| explosion   economic   costs   fast   safety   optimum   yield   compromise |

The rates of reactions in industrial chemical synthesis need to be controlled for two main reasons. Firstly for .... reasons. If the reaction is too .... it could cause an ...., which may injure or even kill employees. Chemical reactions are also controlled for .... reasons. Companies usually choose .... conditions. These will usually involve a .... between the ...., rate of reaction and production ....

Q3 The graph shows the results from an experiment using **magnesium** and dilute **hydrochloric acid**. The **volume of gas** produced was measured at regular intervals as the reaction proceeded.

a) Which reaction was **faster**, P or Q?

....

b) Which reaction produced the **largest volume of gas**, P, Q or R?

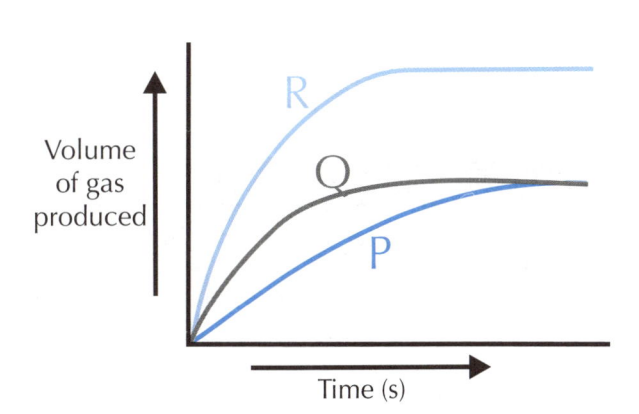

....

c) On the curve for reaction R, mark with an **X** the point where the reaction finishes.

Module C6 — Chemical Synthesis

Rates of Reaction

Q4 Circle the correct words to complete the sentences below.

a) The **higher** / lower the temperature, the faster the rate of reaction.

b) A higher / **lower** concentration will reduce the rate of reaction.

c) A smaller particle size **increases** / decreases the rate of reaction.

d) Using a catalyst **increases** / decreases the rate of reaction.

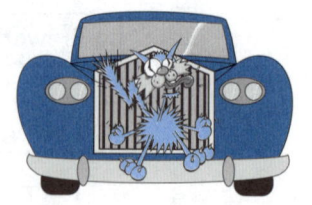

Nora's reactions were slow in the cold.

Q5 In an experiment to investigate **reaction rates**, strips of **magnesium** were put into tubes containing different concentrations of **hydrochloric acid**. The time taken for the magnesium to 'disappear' was measured. The results are shown in the table.

Conc. of acid (g/dm^3)	Time taken (s)
0.3	298
1.0	110
1.5	70
3.0	37
5.0	20
7.0	15

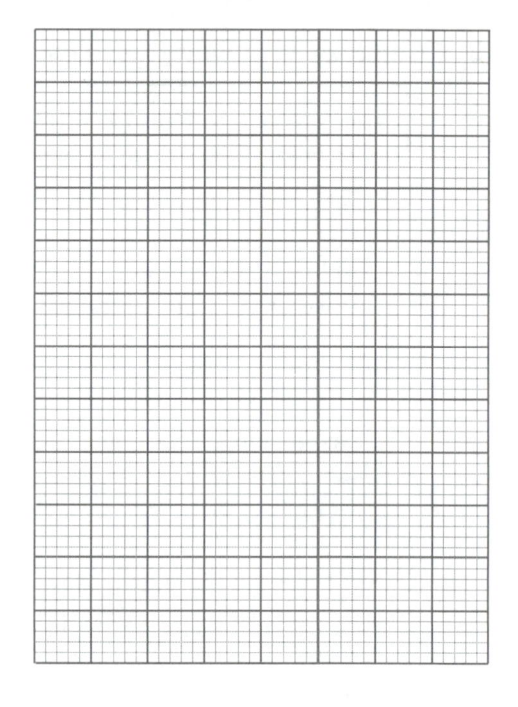

a) Circle **three** things that should be kept the same in each case to make this a **fair test**.

the volume of acid used   what you had for breakfast   the temperature the reaction is carried out at   what colour jumper you're wearing   the size of the magnesium strips used

b) Plot a graph of the data on the grid provided, with concentration of acid on the horizontal axis and time on the vertical axis.

c) What do the results tell you about how the concentration of acid affects the rate of the reaction?

....

d) Complete the following sentence by circling the correct word(s).

If powdered magnesium was used instead of strips of magnesium, the rate of reaction would stay the same / decrease / **increase**.

Top Tips: It's a pretty good idea to learn the four things that reaction rate depends on (temperature, concentration, surface area and catalysts). It's an even better idea to learn exactly how these four things affect the rate of a reaction and what happens when you change them.

Module C6 — Chemical Synthesis

Measuring Rates of Reaction

Q1 Complete the following sentence by circling the correct word from each pair.

> The **speed** / **volume** of a reaction can be measured by observing either how quickly the **products** / **reactants** are used up or how quickly the **products** / **reactants** are formed.

Q2 Charlie was comparing the rate of reaction of 5 g of magnesium ribbon with 20 ml of **five different concentrations** of hydrochloric acid. Each time he measured the volume of **gas** that was produced during the **first minute** of the reaction.

  a) In the space below draw the apparatus that Charlie could use to measure the **volume** of gas produced.

  b) Describe what Charlie could do if he wanted to follow the rate of reaction by calculating the change in **mass** over the course of the reaction.

  ....

  ....

  ....

Q3 Horatio was investigating the reaction between **lead nitrate** and different concentrations of **hydrochloric acid**. When lead nitrate and hydrochloric acid react they produce **lead chloride**, which is an **insoluble solid**.

  a) What name is given to this type of reaction? Circle the correct answer.

  thermal decomposition   precipitation   neutralisation

  b) Describe how Horatio could measure the rate of reaction.

  ....

  ....

  ....

Module C6 — Chemical Synthesis

Module P6 — The Wave Model of Radiation

Waves — The Basics

Q1 Complete the sentence below by circling the correct word in each pair.

Waves transfer **energy** / matter without transferring any energy / **matter**.

Q2 All waves have a **frequency** and a **wavelength**.

a) Circle the units used to measure wavelength: hertz   **metres**

b) What does it mean to say that "the frequency of a wave is 25 hertz"?

....

c) The diagram shows a waveform. Which of A, B and C shows its **wavelength**?

....

Q3 You can make **two types** of wave on a **slinky** spring.

a) Which diagram shows a **transverse** wave and which shows a **longitudinal** wave?

Transverse: ....

Longitudinal: ....

b) Describe one difference between these two types of wave.

....

Q4 Jason draws the graph on the right to show a wave with an **amplitude** of **4 m** and a **wavelength** of **2 m**.

a) What has Jason done wrong? Tick the correct box.

☐ He's drawn an amplitude of 2 m.

☐ He's drawn a wavelength of 4 m.

b) On the same set of axes, draw a wave with a **wavelength** of **5 m** and an **amplitude** of **3 m**.

Q5 A pebble is dropped into still water. Waves move out across the surface of the water. The wavelength is **1.6 cm** and the waves are generated at a rate of **10 a second**.

a) What is the **frequency** of the waves in Hz? ....

b) Calculate the **speed** of the waves. ....

Module P6 — The Wave Model of Radiation

Wave Properties

Q1 Harriet spends at least an hour looking at herself in a **mirror** every day. The image she sees is formed from light reflected by the mirror.

a) What is meant by a 'normal' when talking about reflection?

☐ A line parallel to the surface.

☐ A line at right angles to the surface.

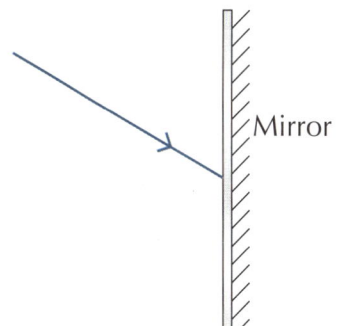

b) Complete the diagram to show the incident ray of light being reflected by the mirror. Label the **angle of incidence**, **i**, the **normal**, and the **angle of reflection**, **r**.

Q2 When a wave passes into a different substance, it may change **speed**. Cross out words in the statements below to make them correct.

a) When a wave slows down, its wavelength **gets longer / gets shorter / stays the same**. The frequency **increases / decreases / stays the same**. The wave may bend **towards / away from** the normal.

b) When a wave speeds up, its the wavelength **gets longer / gets shorter / stays the same**. The frequency **increases / decreases / stays the same**. The wave may bend **towards / away from** the normal.

Q3 The diagram shows a light ray passing through **air** and through **glass**.

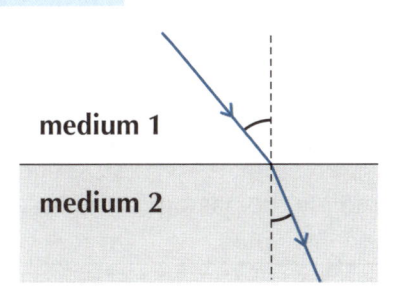

Remember, glass is denser than air.

a) Circle the correct word(s) in each pair to complete the passage.

Medium 1 in the diagram is **glass / air** and medium 2 is **glass / air**.

Light travels **more slowly / faster** in air than in glass, so it will bend

towards / away from the normal as it passes into glass.

b) Sound waves travel faster in glass than in air. Would a sound wave bend **towards** or **away from** the normal as it passes from medium 1 to medium 2? ....

Module P6 — The Wave Model of Radiation

Wave Properties

Q4 Diagrams A and B show plane **water waves** travelling from **deep** to **shallow** water in a ripple tank.

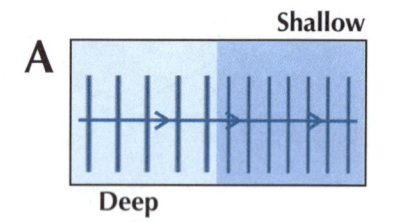

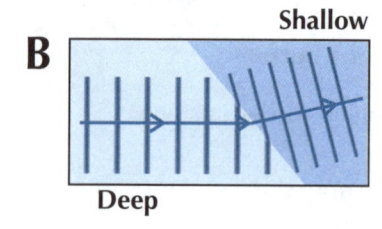

A Shallow / Deep

B Shallow / Deep

a) Which diagram shows the waves being **refracted**? ....

Think about how the waves hit the boundary.

b) Why does refraction **not happen** in the other diagram?

....

c) As the waves pass into shallower water, what happens to their:

i) wavelength? ....

ii) frequency? ....

iii) speed? ....

d) Complete this diagram to show a water wave passing from shallow to **deeper water**.

Think about wavelength, frequency and speed.

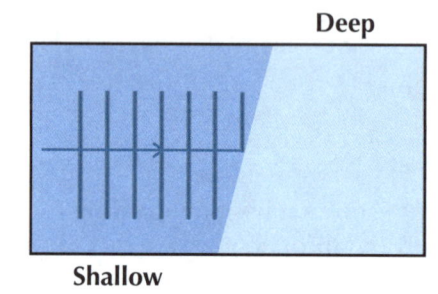

Deep / Shallow

Q5 Emma is doing her homework, which is about **total internal reflection**.

a) Use the words in the box to complete the passage about total internal reflection.

| less dense | boundary | passing | completely | dense |

Total internal reflection means that a wave is .... reflected at the .... as it moves from a .... substance towards a .... substance.

b) In which of these situations could total internal reflection occur? Circle the correct letter(s).

 A Light is shining through air towards water.

 B Light is shining though glass towards air.

Module P6 — The Wave Model of Radiation

Wave Properties

Q6 Circle the correct word(s) from each pair to complete the sentence below.

The critical angle is the angle of incidence / refraction above which a ray from the

less dense / denser medium hitting the boundary will be totally incidentally / internally reflected.

Q7 The critical angle for glass/air is 42°.

Complete the ray diagrams below.

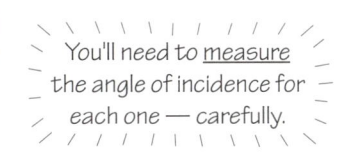

You'll need to measure the angle of incidence for each one — carefully.

Critical angle at toe/banana boundary: 87°

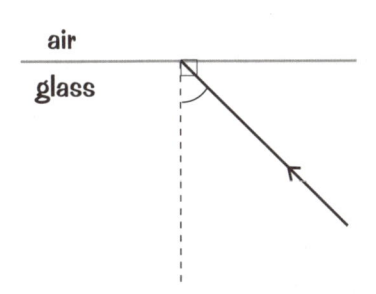

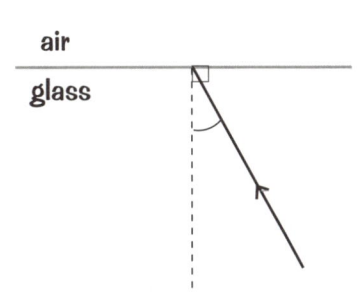

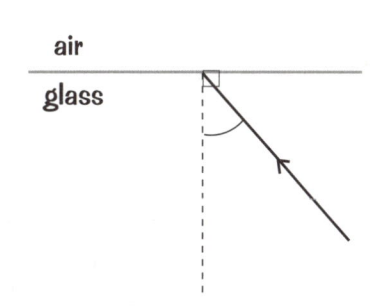

Q8 Another important property of waves is **diffraction**.

a) Explain what diffraction is and when it occurs.

   ....

   ....

b) A ripple tank is used to study the behaviour of water waves as they pass through gaps. The gap in diagram 1 is about the **same size** as the wavelength. The gap in diagram 2 is **much bigger**. Complete both diagrams to show what happens to the waves after they pass through the gaps.

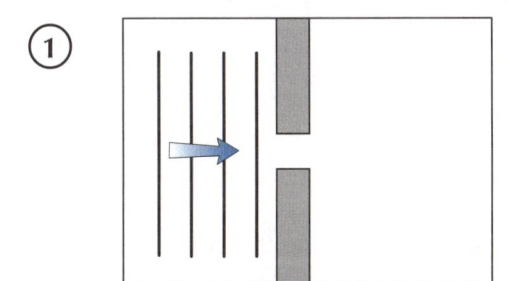

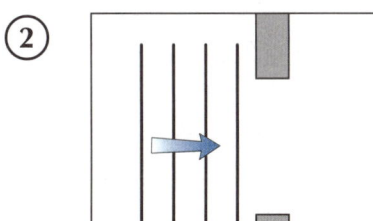

c) **Light waves** have very short wavelengths (about 0.0005 mm).
   Explain why light does not diffract when it shines through a window.

   ....

Top Tips: Wave questions often involve changes in **density**. You need to know how density changes affect wave **speed** — so you can work out if a wave refracts (and if so, which way) or is totally internally reflected. And don't forget that waves **diffract** too — but that's nothing to do with density.

Module P6 — The Wave Model of Radiation

Wave Interference

Q1 The diagrams below both show **displacement–time graphs** of two waves that are **overlapping**.

On each set of empty axes, draw what the graph of the **combined wave** would look like.
Also decide whether the interference is **constructive** or **destructive** — circle the correct answer.

a)

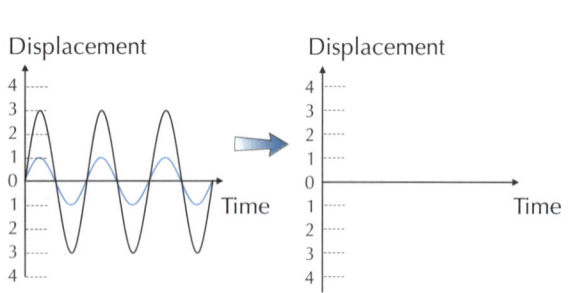

This is **constructive / destructive** interference.

b)

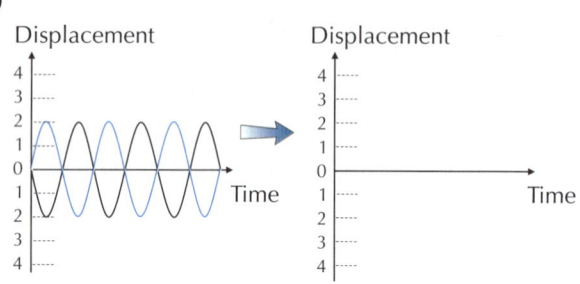

This is **constructive / destructive** interference.

Q2 **Laser light** was shone onto a screen through two very **thin slits** that were close together. A series of bright and dark bands appeared on the screen.

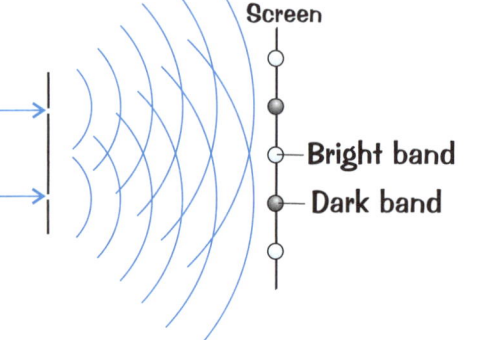

a) What caused the bright bands of light to appear on the screen? Circle the correct answer.

constructive interference   reflection   refraction   destructive interference

b) What is meant by path difference? Tick the box next to the correct answer.

The distance between the starting points of two waves. ☐

The difference in the distance travelled by two waves. ☐

The distance between pairs of interfering waves. ☐

c) Which of these situations would give **destructive** interference? Circle the correct letter.

A A path difference of an odd number of whole wavelengths

B A path difference of an odd number of half wavelengths

C A path difference of an even number of half wavelengths.

d) How would you expect the distance between the bright bands to change if light with a **larger** wavelength was used?

Remember that path difference depends on the wavelength.

Module P6 — The Wave Model of Radiation

Wave Interference

Q3 The diagram shows sets of overlapping water waves produced by two dippers (d1 and d2) in a ripple tank. The **solid lines** indicate where there is a **peak** (or crest) and the **dashed lines** indicate where there is a **trough**.

a) For each point A–D decide whether there will be **constructive** or **destructive** interference. Underline the correct answer.

   A constructive / destructive   B constructive / destructive

   C constructive / destructive   D constructive / destructive

b) The wavelength of the waves is **1 cm**. A point, P, is 5 cm away from d1 and 8 cm away from d2.

   i) Put a circle around the **path difference** at point P.   *Point P is not on the diagram, by the way.*

       1 cm   2 cm   3 cm   4 cm   5 cm

   ii) How many **half wavelengths** fit into this path difference?

   ....

   iii) Will there be **constructive** or **destructive** interference at point P?

   ....

c) The dippers were slowed down to produce a wavelength of 2 cm.

   i) Put a circle around what the **path difference** is at point P now.

       1 cm   2 cm   3 cm   4 cm   5 cm

   ii) How many **half wavelengths** fit into this path difference?

   ....

   iii) Will there be **constructive** or **destructive** interference at point P?

   ....

Q4 Complete the passage below on the nature of **light**.

negative neutral wave light reinforce cancel dark interference positive particle
Overlapping waves may produce .... patterns. This happens because .... and .... parts of two waves can combine to .... each other or cancel each other out. Light beams can interfere, giving a pattern of .... and .... regions. This shows that light can act as a ....

Module P6 — The Wave Model of Radiation

Electromagnetic Radiation

Q1 Indicate whether the following statements are **true** or **false**.

a) Visible light travels faster in a vacuum than both X-rays and radio waves.

b) The higher the frequency of a wave, the longer the wavelength.

c) Radio waves have the shortest wavelength of all EM (electromagnetic) waves.

d) Blue light has a shorter wavelength than red light.

Q2 Complete the table to show the seven types of EM wave.

			VISIBLE LIGHT			Gamma rays

Q3 A beam of EM radiation can be thought of as being made up of waves or **photons**.

a) What are photons?

....

b) Complete the following sentence by filling in the missing words.

The higher the .... of the radiation,
the .... the amount of energy carried by each photon.

Q4 Trevor says, "Why can't we **hear** the Sun when we can see the **light** it emits?"

Why isn't it possible for sound waves from the Sun to travel through space?

Think — what is space?

....

....

Q5 The 'strength' of a beam of light is given by its **intensity**.

a) Which of the following is the correct definition of the intensity of a beam of EM radiation?

    A   The number of waves arriving every second.

    B   The number of photons arriving every second.

    C   The amount of energy delivered per second.

b) What **two things** does the intensity of a beam of radiation depend on?

....

Module P6 — The Wave Model of Radiation

Uses of EM Waves

Q1 X-rays are a type of EM radiation.

a) Complete the paragraph below, choosing from the words in the box.

| bones | flesh | dense | more | less | shadow | absorb | light | diffract | ionising |

Hospitals use X-rays to produce .... pictures to see if a patient has any broken bones. X-rays cannot pass easily through .... materials like .... and metal — these materials .... most of the X-rays. .... is .... dense, so it lets X-rays through more easily.

b) Write down one other use of X-rays.

....

Q2 Information can be transmitted quickly through optical fibres.

a) Which of the following types of EM radiation are used in optical fibres? Circle the correct answer(s).

    Radio   Microwaves   Visible Light   Ultraviolet   Infrared

b) Complete this sentence to explain how optical fibres work, by circling the correct words.

> Optical fibres are made of plastic or glass / metal. Signals travel along the fibre by repeated refractions / reflections between the walls of the fibre.

c) Apart from speed, give one advantage of using optical fibres to transmit a signal.

....

....

Q3 Radio waves are good for broadcasting signals over large distances.

a) Why is this? Underline the correct answer.

    They don't suffer from interference.   They get absorbed by the Earth's atmosphere.

    They don't get significantly absorbed by the Earth's atmosphere.

b) Apart from radio broadcasts, give one other use of radio waves.

....

....

Module P6 — The Wave Model of Radiation

Uses of EM Waves

Q4 Sharon is heating up some **ready-made curry** in her **microwave** oven. Choose words to complete the passage below explaining how the oven heats up the food.

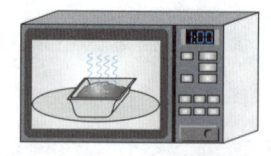

water	reflected	convection	absorbed	kinetic	radiation	conduction

Microwaves are .... by .... molecules in the curry, increasing their .... energy. This energy is then transferred to other parts of the food, mainly by .... and ....

Q5 **Gabrielle** in London calls Carwyn in Toronto using her **satellite phone**.

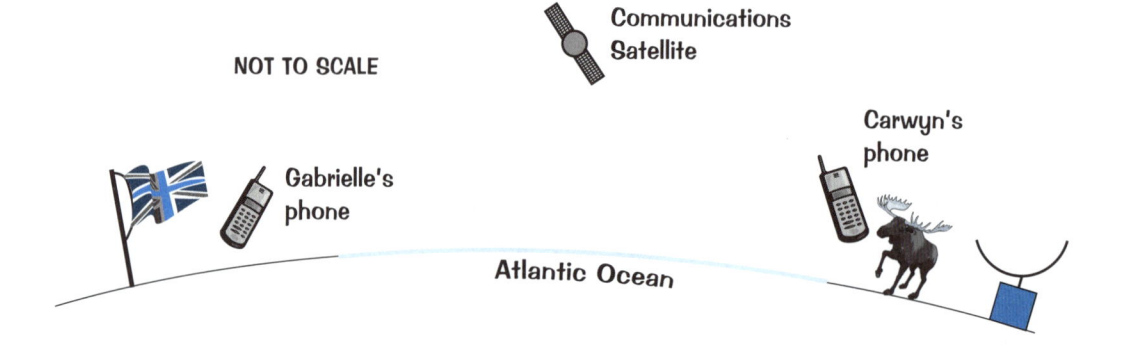

a) Number the following phrases 1 to 7 to explain how the signal reaches Carwyn's phone.

- ☐ The satellite absorbs the signal and then retransmits it to...
- ☐ ...Carwyn's phone.
- ☐ ...a communications satellite...
- ☐ ...near Toronto, which sends the signal to...
- ☐ ...a ground station...
- ☐ ...orbiting above the Earth's atmosphere.
- ☐ [1] Gabrielle's phone sends a microwave signal to...

b) Why are ground-based satellite dishes made of **metal**?

....

c) Why are **microwaves** used to transmit a signal to the satellite?

....

Top Tips: EM waves have a huge number of uses, but luckily you just need to know about six — radio, TV, satellite communications, microwave ovens, X-rays and optical fibres. It's not a short list, so make sure you know what type of wave is used where and, more specifically, why...

Module P6 — The Wave Model of Radiation

Adding Information to Waves

Q1 Complete the passage below using words from the list.

visible light   television   pressure waves   sound waves
EM waves   telephone lines   infrared   signals   X-rays

> For any information to be transmitted, it needs to be converted into
> .... These can be carried along ....
> or broadcast through the air as .... It can also be carried
> using .... or .... waves
> transmitted through optical fibres.

Q2 Liz is listening to DJ Terry on Queenie FM.

a) What do the letters **FM** stand for?

....

b) Indicate whether the following statements about FM radio are **true** or **false**.

	True	False
i) An FM transmitter continually sends out a 'carrier' radio wave.	☐	☐
ii) The signal changes the carrier wave by changing its amplitude.	☐	☐
iii) The signal is carried as changes in frequency of a modulated carrier wave.	☐	☐
iv) The transmitted signal can be picked up by a receiver.	☐	☐

c) What does a radio **receiver** do?

....

....

Q3 Long wavelength radio waves carry signals by **amplitude modulation**.

a) What does amplitude modulation mean?

....

....

b) In the space below, sketch the shape of the **carrier wave** and **signal wave** that produced this shape.

Modulated carrier wave   =   +

                    Carrier wave   Signal wave

Module P6 — The Wave Model of Radiation

Analogue and Digital Signals

Q1 Data can be transmitted either as an **analogue** signal or a **digital** one.

a) What is the difference between an analogue and a digital signal?

....

b) The diagrams below show a 'clean' digital signal and a 'clean' analogue signal. Below each diagram, sketch how the signal might look with 'noise' added to it.

Clean digital signal

Clean analogue signal

The same signal with noise

The same signal with noise

Q2 Fill in the blanks, choosing from the words below.

| digital | analogue | amplified | intensity | weaken | interference | noise |

All signals .... and decrease in .... as they travel. To overcome this, they can be .... Signals may also suffer .... from other signals or from electrical disturbances — causing noise in the signal. When signals are amplified, the noise is also amplified, but it's much harder to remove noise from a(n) .... signal.

Q3 Give **two** advantages of using **digital** signals for communications between two computers which are thousands of kilometres apart.

1. ....

2. ....

Module P6 — The Wave Model of Radiation

Broadband and Wireless Internet

Q1   Read the passage below and answer the questions that follow.

Broadband brings media to the masses

Broadband internet connections are becoming increasingly popular in rich countries such as the USA, Japan and the countries of Europe. Broadband allows more information to be sent and received per second than old-fashioned 'dial-up' internet connections, and is therefore much better suited to downloading entertainment media like music and movies.

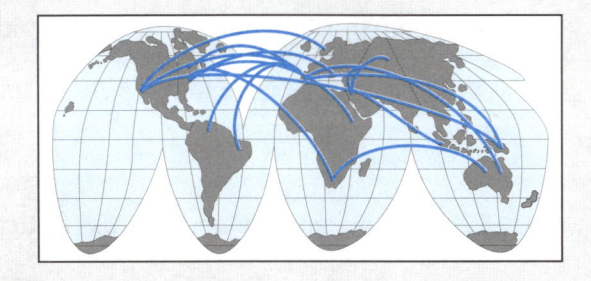

More than 14 million households in the UK have access to the internet (out of the country's 25 million or so households). Of these, approximately 75% have broadband.

There are two main types of broadband internet connection — DSL and cable. DSL involves information being sent along conventional (copper) phone lines, whereas cable connections use a combination of coaxial cable (a cable containing two conducting layers to reduce signal interference) and optical fibres.

Another popular piece of internet technology is known as a wireless router.

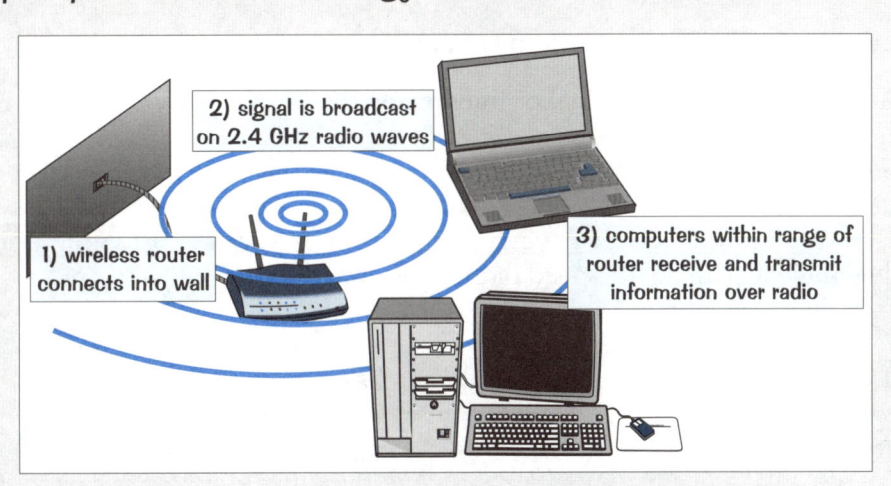

1) wireless router connects into wall
2) signal is broadcast on 2.4 GHz radio waves
3) computers within range of router receive and transmit information over radio

Wireless routers are plugged into a wall socket to gain access to the internet using the normal connection (whether it's via cable, DSL, or anything else). They then transmit the internet connection over a limited range (about 100 metres) using radio waves. Any computer within the range of the router can then communicate with it via radio, allowing users to use the internet without having their computer plugged into a wall socket. The radio waves typically used by wireless routers have a frequency of about 2.4 GHz (2 400 000 000 Hz).

a)   Using information from the article, suggest why broadband internet connections are becoming more popular.

....

....

Module P6 — The Wave Model of Radiation

Broadband and Wireless Internet

b) i) Using information from the article, estimate the **percentage** of UK households that have access to an internet connection.

   ....

   ii) Approximately how many households in the UK have a **broadband** internet connection?

   ....

c) Cable broadband connections use **optical fibres** like the one shown below.

   i) In the diagram, which of the two labelled layers (A or B) is the **denser**? ....

   ii) In which material, A or B, would light travel **faster**? ....

d) **Wireless routers** use radio waves to communicate with computers.

   i) Are radio waves **longitudinal** or **transverse**?

   ....

   ii) The wavelength of a typical wireless router's radio waves is 0.125 m. Using information from the article, calculate the speed of the radio waves.

   ....

   ....

   ....

   iii) Circle the type of signal that the router's radio waves are likely to carry.

                            digital   analogue

e) Wireless routers are sometimes used to provide internet access for an entire building, but they are also commonly used in individual households in tightly packed residential areas. Suggest why this might lead to **security** problems.

....

....

....

Module P6 — The Wave Model of Radiation

CGP

GCSE
Additional Science

OCR 21st Century

Answer Book
Foundation Level

Contents

Module B4 — Homeostasis 3

Module C4 — Chemical Patterns 4

Module P4 — Explaining Motion 6

Module B5 — Growth and Development 8

Module C5 — Chemicals of the Natural Environment 9

Module P5 — Electric Circuits 10

Module B6 — Brain and Mind 13

Module C6 — Chemical Synthesis 14

Module P6 — The Wave Model of Radiation 17

Published by Coordination Group Publications Ltd.

ISBN: 978 1 84762 005 7

Groovy website: www.cgpbooks.co.uk
Printed by Elanders Hindson Ltd, Newcastle upon Tyne.
Jolly bits of clipart from CorelDRAW®
Text, design, layout and original illustrations © Coordination Group Publications Ltd. 2007
All rights reserved.

Module B4 — Homeostasis

Module B4 — Homeostasis

Page 1 — The Basics of Homeostasis

Q1 a) constant, changing, function, constant
b) E.g. body temperature and water content

Q2 a)

Temperature	(increases) decreases
Water content	increases / (decreases)

b) A decrease in core body temperature / hypothermia.

Q3 receptors — detect stimuli
processing centres — receive information and coordinate a response
effectors — produce a response

Pages 2-3 — Diffusion and Osmosis

Q1 random, higher, lower, bigger
Q2 a) In the blood.
b) i) oxygen
ii) carbon dioxide
Q3 a) False
b) False
c) False
d) True
Q4 water, partially, membrane, dilute, concentrated, diffusion
Q5 a) B
b) fall, B, A
c) A membrane that only allows certain substances to diffuse through it.

Page 4 — Enzymes

Q1 a) They're proteins.
They speed up chemical reactions.
They're biological catalysts.
b) E.g.

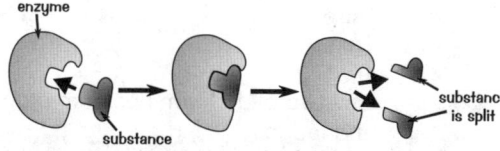

Q2 a) 35 °C (one degree either way acceptable)
b) frequency/energy, energy/frequency, increases
c) They are denatured/they stop working.

Pages 5-6 — Controlling Body Temperature

Q1 a) Heat energy loss and heat energy gain.
b) i) skin
ii) brain
c) brain, effectors, muscles/sweat glands, sweat glands/muscles

Q2 a) i) sweating
ii) Too much water loss through sweating can cause dehydration.
b) i) the muscles
ii) rapidly, increasing, tissue

Q3 a) Any two of, e.g. a hot climate / physical exertion / extensive burns / dehydration.
b) Dizziness, headaches and confusion should be circled.
c) The normal mechanisms stop working.
d) The patient would be cooled down by being placed in a cool/air-conditioned room. They would be given cold water to drink and be bathed in cool water.

Q4 a) hypothermia
b) Any four of, e.g. shivering / low energy / confusion / slurred speech / apprehension / loss of control of limbs/extremities / memory loss / unconsciousness.
c) Warm, dry clothing
Warmed by a gentle heat source

Pages 7-8 — Controlling Water Content

Q1 a) In food / in drinks / from respiration.
b) Any three of, e.g. sweating / breathing / in faeces / in urine
c) A balanced water level is important for maintaining the concentration of cell contents at the correct level for cell activity/ to maintain cell function.

Q2 a) more, increase, more
b) more, faster, more
c) more, less

Q3 salt/water/sugar/urea, salt/water/sugar/urea, salt/water/sugar/urea, salt/water/sugar/urea, sugar, salt/water, salt/water, bladder

Q4 a) E.g. exercise / external temperature / intake of fluids and salts.
b) i) true
ii) false
iii) true
iv) true
v) false

Q5 a) less, larger, dilute, dehydration
b) i) E.g. ecstasy
ii) E.g. it can result in a smaller amount of more concentrated urine (than normal) being produced.

Pages 9-10 — Treating Kidney Failure

Q1 a) i) proteins and red blood cells
ii) They are too big to pass through the membrane.
iii) urea

Module C4 — Chemical Patterns

iv) It is equal, to prevent the diffusion of glucose/sugar out of the bloodstream and into the dialysis fluid. The amount of sugar in the patient's blood should remain the same.

b) 1. A needle is inserted into a blood vessel in the patient's arm to remove blood.
2. The patient's blood flows into the dialysis machine and between partially permeable membranes.
3. Excess water, ions and wastes are filtered out of the blood and pass into the dialysis fluid.
4. Dialysis continues until nearly all the waste and excess substances are removed.
5. Blood is returned to the patient's body via a vein in their arm.

c) i) E.g. it is a long-term cure / it removes the need for frequent dialysis, which is time-consuming.
ii) E.g. a kidney that is a good tissue match is used / the patient is given drugs to suppress their immune system.

Module C4 — Chemical Patterns
Page 11 — Atoms

Q1 neutron — It's heavy and has no charge.
nucleus — It's in the centre of the atom and contains protons and neutrons.
electron — It moves around the nucleus in shells.

Q2 neutron/proton
proton/neutron
electron

Q3

Particle	Mass	Charge
Proton	1	+1
Neutron	1	0
Electron	0.0005	−1

Page 12 — Atoms in Chemical Reactions

Q1 a) 0
b) ion
c) the same
d) negatively
e) protons

Q2

element	electrons	protons
magnesium	12	12
carbon	6	6
oxygen	8	8

Q3 a) i) (l)
ii) (g)
b) Reactants: sodium and water
Products: sodium hydroxide and hydrogen
c) sodium + water → sodium hydroxide + hydrogen

Page 13 — Line Spectrums

Q1 a) colour, flame
b) yellow/orange — sodium
red — lithium
lilac — potassium

Q2 a) electrons, excited, light, light, line, elements, light, electron, element, line
b) They have been used to discover new elements.

Pages 14-15 — The Periodic Table

Q1 a) Any one of: sodium, magnesium, aluminium, phosphorus, sulfur, chlorine, argon.
b) Any one of: lithium, sodium, rubidium, caesium, francium.
c) Any one of: fluorine, chlorine, bromine, iodine, astatine.
d) Any one of: lithium, sodium, potassium, rubidium, caesium, francium.

Q2

Name	Symbol	Relative atomic mass	Proton number
Iron	Fe	56	26
Lead	Pb	207	82
Xenon	Xe	131	54
Copper	Cu	63.5	29

Q3 a) vertical
b) metals
c) increasing
d) right-hand
e) similar

Q4 a) True
b) True
c) False
d) True
e) True

Q5 Any two of: helium, neon, krypton, xenon and radon.

Q6 a) The following should be ticked: **A** and **D**
b) Fluorine and chlorine are in the same group.

Page 16 — Electron Shells

Q1 a) True
b) False
c) True
d) False

Q2 There should be two electrons in the inner shell. The outer shell contains too many electrons.

Module C4 — Chemical Patterns

Q3 a) 2, 2
b) 2, 6
c) 2, 8, 4
d) 2, 8, 8, 2
e) 2, 8, 3
f) 2, 8, 8
Q4 a) 2, 8, 7
b)

Q4

Increases down the group	Decreases down the group
the melting points of the halogens	the reactivity of the halogens
the boiling points of the halogens	

Q5 a) sodium bromide
b) i) Faster, because iodine is less reactive than bromine.
ii) Slower, because chlorine is more reactive than bromine.
Q6 a) Bromine is less reactive than chlorine so it doesn't displace it from the potassium chloride solution.
b) bromine + potassium chloride → potassium bromide + iodine
c) No, because fluorine is more reactive than bromine, and so it won't displace the fluorine from potassium fluoride.

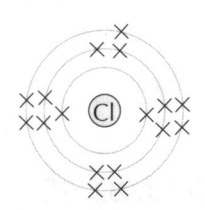

Page 17 — Group 1 — Alkali Metals

Q1 a)

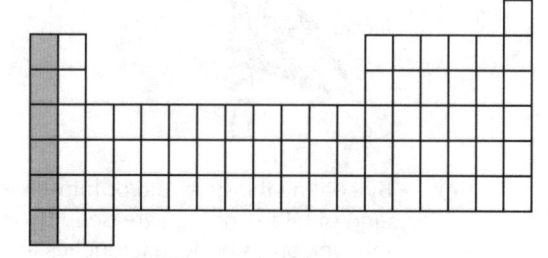

b) (least) lithium (Li), sodium (Na), potassium (K) (most).
c) shiny, tarnish
Q2 one, sodium hydroxide, hydrogen
Q3 a) Lithium is less dense than water.
b) lithium hydroxide — alkaline
c) i) sodium + water → sodium hydroxide + hydrogen
ii) More vigorous — sodium is more reactive as it's further down the group.

Page 20 — Laboratory Safety

Q1 a) oxidising
b) highly flammable
c) toxic
d) harmful
e) irritant
f) corrosive
Q2 a) True
b) False
c) True
d) False
Q3 a) Fluorine and chlorine are poisonous gases at room temperature and the other halogens have poisonous vapours.
b) Corrosive substances attack and destroy living tissue and other substances, e.g. metals.

Pages 18-19 — Group 7 — Halogens

Q1

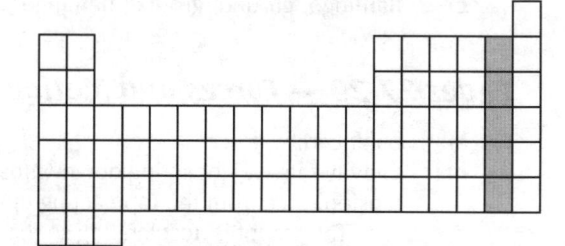

Q2 fluorine — F — yellow gas — most reactive
chlorine — Cl — green gas — very reactive
bromine — Br — red-brown liquid — quite reactive
iodine — I — grey solid — least reactive
Q3 a) False
b) True
c) True
d) True

Page 21 — Ionic Bonding

Q1 a) electrons, ions
b) charged particles
c) attracted to
Q2 a) one
b) positive/+1
c) NaCl
Q3 a) True
b) False
c) True
d) True
e) False

Module P4 — Explaining Motion

Module P4 — Explaining Motion

Page 22 — Speed

Q1 a) True
b) False
c) True

Q2 a) **Snail 1** — its d-t graph has the steepest gradient.
b) speed = distance ÷ time = 0.5 ÷ 40 = **0.0125 m/s**

Q3 a) 5 minutes = 5 × 60 = **300 s**
b) $\text{Speed} = \dfrac{\text{distance}}{\text{time}} = \dfrac{1500}{300} = \mathbf{5\ m/s}$.
c) average

Q4 a) 3 × 2 m = **6 m**
b) 6 ÷ 0.2 = **30 m/s**.
c) Yes

Pages 23-24 — Speed and Velocity

Q1 a) False
b) True
c) True
d) False

Q2 −3 m

Q3 a) speed = distance ÷ time = 3000 ÷ 300 = **10 m/s**.
b) [graph showing Hare and Tortoise distance vs time]
c) After **600 s / 10 minutes** (read off from the graph where the two lines cross).

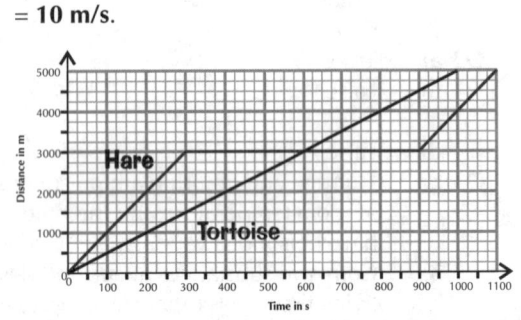

Q4 a) 180 s (or 3 mins)
b) 450 m
c) He runs there in half the time it took him to walk there — 90 s. See graph:
[distance-time graph]

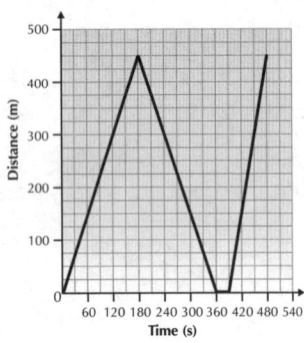

Q5 a) False
b) False
c) True
d) False

Page 25 — Velocity

Q1 A — (constant) acceleration (from 0 - 3 m/s)
B — constant speed/velocity (of 3 m/s)
C — (constant) acceleration (from 3 - 9 m/s)
D — constant speed/velocity (of 9 m/s)
E — (constant) deceleration (from 9 - 7 m/s)

Q2 −12 m/s

Q3 Line A = Line 3
Line B = Line 1
Line C = Line 2

Page 26 — Forces and Friction

Q1 force, interaction, 150, equal, opposite

Q2 a) The surface of the slide and the penguin's back.
b) [diagram of penguin on slide with friction arrow]
c) By coating the slide and/or himself in some kind of lubricant (e.g. grease). / By reducing the area of his body that touches the slide.

Q3 jet engine, a force, an equal, jet engine, forwards

Q4 a) Weight
b) [diagram of flamingo with forces A and B labelled]
c) flamingo, ground, ground, flamingo

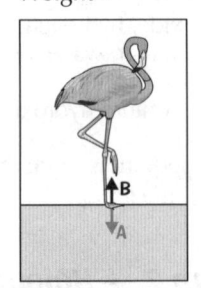

Pages 27-29 — Forces and Motion

Q1 a) balanced by, force
b) Gravity / its weight acting downwards and a tension force from the rope acting upwards.
c) No. The teapot is accelerating so the forces cannot be balanced.

Q2 a) [diagram of cyclist with Reaction (up), Thrust (left arrow shown), Drag / air resistance (and friction between tyres and ground etc.), Weight (down)]
b) No — he is decelerating.
South / backwards.

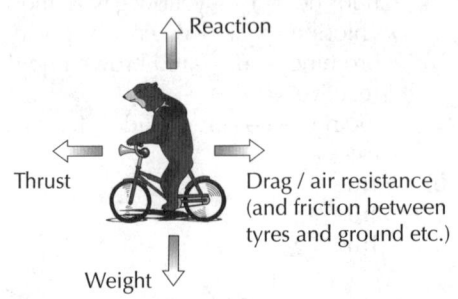

Module P4 — Explaining Motion

Q3 a) Statement **D** should be circled.
b) i) The thrust is **less than** the drag.
ii) The lift is **less than** the weight.
Q4 a) 1 500 000 – 1 500 000 = **0 N**
b) 6 000 000 – 1 500 000 = **4 500 000 N**
Q5 **X** = unbalanced force of gravity.
Y = forces in balance.
Z = reaction force from ground acts.
Q6 Truck A's momentum = 30 × 3000
= 90 000 kg m/s.
Truck B's momentum = 10 × 4500
= 45 000 kg m/s.
Truck C's momentum = 20 × 4000
= 80 000 kg m/s.
Truck D's momentum = 15 × 3500
= 52 500 kg m/s.
So the order of increasing momentum is:
B, D, C, A.
Q7 a) Change in momentum = resultant force × time.
b) 8000 × 1.2 = **9600 kg m/s**
c) Larger (if the time period was shorter for the same change in momentum, the resultant force must have been larger than 8000 N).
Q8 a) increases, decreases/reduces
b) E.g. crumple zones, air bags.
Q9 a) 1200 × 30 = **36 000 kg m/s**
b) C

Page 30 — Work

Q1 a) Work involves the transfer of **energy**.
b) To do work a **force** acts over a **distance**.
c) Work is measured in **joules**.
Q2 a) True
b) True
c) False
d) True
Q3 a) Work done = force × distance
= 1200 × 8 = **9600 J**
b) From the chemical energy in its food.
c) Heat energy (because of friction between the donkey's feet and the surface of the track) and some sound energy.
Q4 a) gravity / his weight
b) Distance moved = 10 × 20 cm
= 200 cm = 2 m.
So work done = 600 × 2 = **1200 J**.

Page 31 — Kinetic Energy

Q1 a) doubled
b) quadrupled
Q2 K.E. = ½mv² = ½ × 200 × (9)²
= 0.5 × 200 × 81 = **8100 J**
Q3 The vehicles should be numbered, from left to right, **1, 3, 2**.
Q4 a) The pushing force does work on the bicycle and increases its kinetic energy.
b) Jack and his bicycle gain 50 J of kinetic energy. Jack's dad loses 50 J of energy.

Pages 32-33 — Gravitational Potential Energy

Q1 a) the 10 kg dumbbell
b) decreases
Q2 a) G.P.E. = 250 × 1.2 = **300 J**
b) Total G.P.E. = 28 × 300 J = **8400 J**
c) The energy transferred and the work done by Fred are the same thing, so **8400 J**.
Q3 a) A — maximum G.P.E.
B — G.P.E. is being converted to K.E.
C — minimum G.P.E., maximum K.E.
D — K.E. is being converted to G.P.E.
b) i) At half the height, half the potential energy should have been converted into kinetic energy, i.e. **150 kJ**.
ii) It will be slowed down by frictional forces, etc.
Q4 Just before the ball hits the ground, it has converted all its gravitational potential energy into kinetic energy, so it has **121 J** of kinetic energy.
Q5 a) G.P.E. = weight × height
= 500 × 8 = **4000 J**
b) The energy converted from potential energy to kinetic energy is 1500 J, so the difference must be the wasted energy. 4000 J – 1500 J = **2500 J**.
c) friction and air resistance/drag
Q6 a) Work done = change in energy. Change in G.P.E = weight × change in height
= 700 × 20 = **14 000 J**
b) **14 000 J** (All her gravitational potential energy is converted into kinetic energy.)

Pages 34-35 — Bungee Jumping

Q1 a) i) constant speed (downwards)
ii) momentarily stationary / accelerating upwards
b) i) gravity, tension
ii) tension
c) 200 ÷ 50 = **4 times**
d) Speed = distance ÷ time
= 200 ÷ 10 = **20 m/s**
e) Momentum = mass × velocity
= 75 × 55 = **4125 kg m/s**
f) Work done = force × distance
= 950 × 233 = **221 350 J**
g) A skydiver will stop accelerating when the upward force (air resistance) acting on them is equal to the downward force (due to gravity/their weight). Their maximum speed is limited by the air resistance.

Module B5 — Growth and Development

Module B5 — Growth and Development

Page 36 — DNA — Making Proteins

Q1 a) True
   b) False
   c) True
   d) False
Q2 a) It provides the instructions needed to make all the proteins in the body.
   b) double helix
   c) four
Q3

```
A G G C T A G C C A A T C G C C G A A G C T C A
T C C G A T C G G T T A G C G G C T T C G A G T
```

Q4 ribosomes, cytoplasm, ribosomes, nucleus, messenger, ribosomes

Page 37 — Cell Division — Mitosis

Q1 a) True
   b) False
   c) True
   d) True
   e) True
   f) False
Q2 grows, chromosomes, splits, identical
Q3 a) two
   b) X
   c) centre, Cell fibres
   d) nuclei
   e) cytoplasm

Page 38 — Cell Division — Meiosis

Q1 a) Meiosis
   b) Mitosis, Meiosis
   c) Meiosis
   d) Meiosis
Q2 a) Before the cell starts to divide it duplicates its DNA to produce an exact copy.
   b) For the first meiotic division the chromosomes line up in their pairs across the centre of the cell.
   c) The pairs are pulled apart, so each new cell only has one copy of each type of chromosome.
   d) The chromosomes line up across the centre of the cell ready for the second division, and the left and right arms are pulled apart.
   e) There are now four gametes, each containing half the original number of chromosomes.
Q3 half, chromosomes, fertilisation, zygote, full

Page 39 — Development from a Single Cell

Q1 a) True
   b) False
   c) True
   d) False
   e) False
Q2 a) The process by which a cell changes to become specialised for a job.
   b) Cells that can develop into different types of cell depending on what instructions they get.
Q3 eight, genes, active, proteins
Q4 The following should be circled:
differentiated cell
gamete
nerve cell
red blood cell
Q5 Embryonic stem cells can differentiate into any type of body cell. Adult stem cells are less versatile — they can only turn into certain types of cell.

Pages 40-41 — Growth in Plants

Q1 Organs: flowers, roots, leaves
Tissues: phloem, xylem
Q2 a) False
   b) False
   c) False
   d) True
Q3 a) A part of a plant that has been cut off.
   b) plant hormones
   c) yes
   d) Cutting 2 would be most likely to grow best as it will contain undifferentiated stem cells in the meristem tissue in the bud. Cutting 1 won't grow as well as it doesn't contain any undifferentiated stem cells.
Q4 E.g. Animals tend to only grow when they are young, but plants grow throughout their lives. Growth in animals happens by cell division, whereas in plants growth in height is mainly due to cell elongation.
Q5 towards, light, away, light, nutrients, sunlight, direction
Q6 a) False
   b) False
   c) False
   d) True
   e) True
   f) True

Page 42 — Stem Cells and Parkinson's

Q1 a) Any three of, e.g. shaking movements / muscle stiffness / difficulty moving / problems with handwriting, speech or balance.

Module C5 — Chemicals of the Natural Environment

b) The stem cells died soon after they were transplanted into the patients' brains.
c) The symptoms of Parkinson's are caused by a lack of dopamine. So by replacing these cells, which produce dopamine, their symptoms will be reduced.

Module C5 — Chemicals of the Natural Environment

Page 43 — Chemicals in the Atmosphere

Q1

substance	element or compound	chemical symbol
oxygen	element	O_2
carbon dioxide	compound	CO_2
argon	element	Ar
nitrogen	element	N_2

Q2 non-metallic, molecular, atoms, strong, weak
Q3 a) low
  b) don't conduct
  c) gases and liquids

Page 44 — Chemicals in the Hydrosphere

Q1 water, dissolved, salts, ions, salty
Q2 strong, positive, negative, large
Q3 a)

	Conducts electricity?
When solid	No
When dissolved in water	Yes

  b) When it is in solution, the ions are free to move about and can carry the electric current. When it is solid the ions are held in place so it can't conduct electricity.

Pages 45-46 — Chemicals in the Lithosphere

Q1 crust, mantle, minerals, aluminium/silicon/oxygen, silicon/oxygen/aluminium, oxygen/aluminium/silicon, elements
Q2 a) Because it has a giant structure where all the atoms are bonded together by strong covalent bonds, which are difficult to break.
  b) Because it doesn't have any free electrons or ions to carry electrical charge.
  c) E.g. hard / insoluble in water
  d) E.g. granite (as quartz) / sandstone.
Q3 uncharged atoms, strong, high, don't, insoluble

Q4 Sample A: sandstone
  Reason: It contains a large percentage composition of silicon.
  Sample B: limestone
  Reason: It contains a large percentage composition of calcium.
Q5 a) E.g. they are attractive.
  b) E.g. they are rare.
  c) All the atoms in diamond are bonded together by strong covalent bonds. It takes a lot of energy to overcome these strong forces.

Page 47 — Chemicals in the Biosphere

Q1 carbon, hydrogen, oxygen, nitrogen, phosphorus, sulfur
Q2 Elements: carbon, hydrogen, oxygen
  Molecular formula: $C_5H_{10}O_5$
Q3 a) Denitrifying bacteria converting nitrates in the soil into nitrogen in the atmosphere.
  b) Nitrogen from plants moving into animals by feeding.

Page 48 — Metals from Minerals

Q1 a) True
  b) False
  c) True
  d) True
Q2 Carbon, below, reduction, electrolysis, more
Q3 a) Carbon (in the wood) is more reactive than copper, so it can 'steal' oxygen from the copper ore.
  b) The reduction of copper happens at easily attainable temperatures.

Pages 49-50 — Electrolysis

Q1 electric, dissolved/molten, molten/dissolved, decompose, taken from, external circuit, given to, molecules
Q2 a) i) G
    ii) B
    iii) E
    iv) C
    v) F
  b) the flow of electrons
Q3 For electricity to flow through the electrolyte, the ions need to be free to move.
Q4 a) True
  b) False
  c) True
  d) True
  e) False

Module P5 — Electric Circuits

Q5 a) i) bauxite
ii) aluminium oxide, Al_2O_3
b) Aluminium is more reactive than carbon so the oxide will not be reduced by carbon.
c) E.g. it is very difficult to extract from its compounds.

Page 51 — Metals

Q1 a) A, B and D
b) Electrical conductivity — element C is not a good conductor of electricity so it can't be a metal.
Q2 a) 3 (it's an excellent conductor of heat, low cost and resistant to corrosion)
b) 2 (it has excellent strength and is resistant to corrosion)
c) 1 (it's very corrosion resistant and very strong)
Q3 a) metallic
b) heat/electricity, heat/electricity, electrons
c) malleable / bendy / ductile

Pages 52-54 — Environmental Impact

Q1 a) Finite resources are resources that can't be replaced. Relying on finite resources could cause problems because they may eventually run out.
b) Any one of, e.g. recycling metal / use less metal / use metal more efficiently / use other materials in place of metals.
Q2 Social factors: any two of, e.g. new jobs available for locals / improved local transport services / influx of people might put strain on local services.
Economic factors: e.g. more money in local economy / more jobs available / more goods made from the extracted metal are available.
Environmental factors: any two of, e.g. pollution such as dust and noise / habitat destruction / scarring of the landscape / deep mine shafts are dangerous if the mine is abandoned / after extraction the area may be turned into a conservation area.
Q3 a) Any two of, e.g. it destroys landscapes. / It destroys habitats. / It produces waste products that must be disposed of. / It causes noise pollution.
b) E.g. it brings money and employment to the area.
c) E.g. many things made of metal cause damage to the environment, e.g. cars burn fossil fuels and produce pollution.
d) i) 31% of 5 billion = 0.31 × 5 000 000 000
= **1 550 000 000 cans**
ii) 42% of 5 billion = 0.42 × 5 000 000 000
= **2 100 000 000 cans**
iii) 2 100 000 000 − 1 550 000 000
= **550 000 000**
e) E.g. the collection service in the area may be poor. / They might not want to make the effort to separate the aluminium from their waste.
f) Any one of, e.g. Recycling aluminium uses only 5% of the energy needed to extract pure aluminium from bauxite. / For every 1 kg of aluminium recycled, 6 kg of bauxite, 4 kg of chemical products and 14 kWh of electricity are saved. / 20 recycled cans can be made with the energy it takes to make just one brand new can.

Module P5 — Electric Circuits

Page 55 — Static Electricity

Q1 Static, insulating, friction, electrons, positive/negative, negative/positive
Q2 Circled: positive and negative, negative and positive
Underlined: positive and positive, negative and negative
Q3 a) True
b) False
c) False
Q4 same, repel, attracted to, build-up, charged

Pages 56-57 — Electric Current

Q1 a) flow, charge
b) Voltage, pushes
c) Resistance
Q2 A — Current — amperes
V — Voltage — volts
Ω — Resistance — ohms
Q3 a) False
b) True
c) True
d) False
Q4 a) Pump — Battery
Pipes — Wires
Water flowing in pipes — Charge
Constriction where it is harder for water to flow — Component
b) Increasing the **voltage** of the power supply.
Q5 a) voltage, charge, increases
b) i) The resistance should be decreased.
ii) The resistance should be increased.
Q6 a) Plastic — Insulator — Charges within material are mostly fixed in position.
Metal — Conductor — Material contains lots of charges that are free to move.
b) electrons

Module P5 — Electric Circuits

Q7 a) Ranjit
b) Lara is wrong because no charge flows when the switch is open and the circuit is incomplete.
Brian is wrong because charge flows through components without being used up.

Page 58 — Circuits — The Basics

Q1 Cell — Provides the 'push' on the charge.
—⊣|—

Variable Resistor — Used to alter the current.

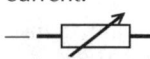

Voltmeter — Measures the voltage.

Ammeter — Measures the current.

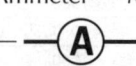

Q2 a) 1. Battery
2. Thermistor
3. Fixed Resistor
4. LDR
5. Switch
6. Filament Lamp
b) Y
Q3 P.D., energy, charge, to, from, voltmeter, parallel

Pages 59-60 — Resistance

Q1 a) True
b) False
c) True
d) False

Q2

Voltage (V)	Current (A)	Resistance (Ω)
6	2	3
8	4	2
9	3	3
4	8	0.5

Q3 current, increases, Filament lamps, high, hot, gives out
Q4 a) False
b) True
c) True
d) False
Q5 a) i) constant
ii) The line is a straight line through the origin.
b) i) 1 A
ii) Resistance = voltage ÷ current
= 2 ÷ 1 = 2 Ω

c) The graph should show a straight line through the origin that is less steep than the original line. E.g.

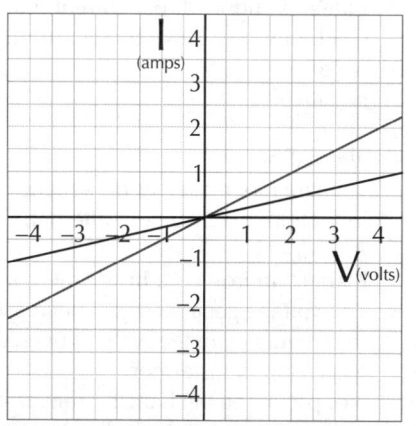

Q6 a) i) LDR
ii) decreases
b) i) A thermistor.
ii) The resistance will start high and gradually decrease as the temperature increases.

Page 61 — Series Circuits

Q1 Same everywhere in the circuit — Current
Shared out between the components — Total potential difference
The sum of the resistances — Total resistance
Can be different for each component — Potential difference
Q2 a) cell
b) resistor R_2
c) i) larger
ii) The battery has to push charges through all of the components. / Because the total resistance is the sum of the individual resistances.
Q3 a) the same
b) different
c) smaller

Page 62 — Parallel Circuits

Q1 a) True
b) True
c) False
Q2 a) stays the same, current, resistance
b) increases, resistance
c) decreases, more
d) stays the same, lamp
Q3 a) 0.27 + 0.43 = 0.7 A
b) R_1 because a smaller current is flowing through it.

Module P5 — Electric Circuits

Pages 63-65 — Mains Electricity

Q1 a) 230 V
b) Batteries supply direct current, mains electricity uses alternating current.
Q2 a) i) negative
ii) negative
b) i) none
ii) alternating
Q3 voltage, moving, electromagnetic induction, magnet, coil, alternating
Q4 a) A
b) Placing an iron core inside the coil.
Q5 a) The voltage generated will decrease. (Also the frequency of the AC will decrease.)
b) a (step-up) transformer
c) No, providing the hamster runs fast enough it doesn't matter which direction it runs in, because the magnetic field will still be changing.
Q6
1. An alternating voltage is connected to the primary coil of a transformer.
2. An alternating current flows in the primary coil.
3. This causes a rapidly changing magnetic field in the core.
4. The changing magnetic field induces an alternating voltage in the secondary coil.
5. An alternating current can flow in a circuit connected to the secondary coil.

Q7 a) A transformer consists of two coils of wire wound around an iron core.
b) i) Step-up transformers have more turns on the secondary coil, whereas step-down transformers have more turns on the primary coil.
ii) Step-up transformers are used to increase the voltage, whereas step-down transformers decrease it.
c) The magnetic field created in the core must be constantly changing in order to induce a voltage in the secondary coil. With direct current, the magnetic field is constant.

Pages 66-67 — Electrical Energy

Q1 a) energy, to, energy, charge
Q2 a) Energy = **power** × **time**
b) i) Energy = 100 × 10 = **1000 J** = 1 kJ
ii) Energy = 500 × (2 × 60) = **60 000 J** = 60 kJ
iii) Energy = (1 × 1000) × 20 = **20 000 J** = 20 kJ
Q3 a) Simon is right.
b) A joule is a very small amount of electrical energy, so kilowatt-hours are often more convenient.

Q4

	Lamp A	Lamp B	Lamp C
Voltage (V)	12	3	230
Current (A)	2.5	4	0.1
Power (W)	30	12	23
Energy used in one minute (J)	1800	720	1380

Q5 a) Energy = (150 ÷ 1000) × 0.5 = **0.075 kWh**
b) Energy = 2.7 × [1 + (15 ÷ 60)] = **3.375 kWh**
c) i) Total energy = 0.075 + 3.375 = **3.45 kWh**
ii) Cost = number of kWh × cost per kWh = 3.45 × 8.5 = 29.325 = **29p**
Q6 a) 100 J
b) 5 J
c) 100 − 5 = **95 J**
d) Efficiency = energy usefully transferred ÷ total energy supplied × 100%
= 5 ÷ 100 × 100% = **5%**

Q7

Total Energy Supplied (J)	Energy Usefully Transferred (J)	Efficiency (%)
2000	1500	75
4000	2000	50
4000	1000	25
600	200	33

Pages 68-69 — The National Grid

Q1 a) Any one of, e.g. it allowed ordinary people to have a supply of electricity to their homes, people could rely on the supply of electricity, people were no longer limited to appliances that matched the voltage of their particular electricity supply, people did not have to live near a power station because electricity could be distributed over longer distances.
ii)
b) AC
c) i) step-up transformer

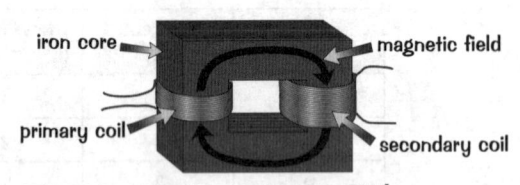

d) i) 370 000 + 30 000 = **400 000 GWh**
ii) $$\text{Efficiency} = \frac{\text{Energy usefully transferred}}{\text{Total energy supplied}} \times 100\%$$

$$\text{Efficiency} = \frac{370\,000}{400\,000} \times 100\% = \mathbf{92.5\%}$$

e) resistance, wastes, resistance

Module B6 — Brain and Mind

Module B6 — Brain and Mind

Pages 70-72 — The Nervous System

Q1 stimulus, change, environment, temperature, respond, favourable, danger, mate

Q2 a) central nervous system
b) The CNS coordinates responses to stimuli.
c) [Diagram of human body with Brain and Spinal cord labelled]
d) i) CNS, rest of the body
ii) sensory neurones and motor neurones
e) i) sensory neurones
ii) motor neurones

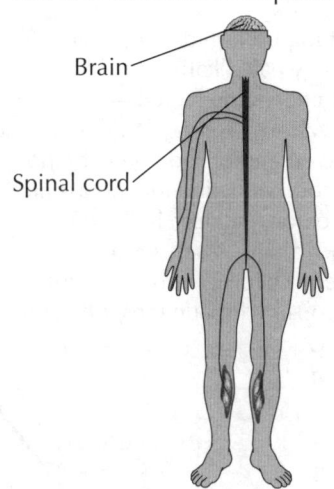

Q3 a) effectors — respond to nerve impulses, bring about a change.
receptors — detect stimuli

	Example	Make up part of...
Receptor	taste buds	the tongue
	sound receptor cells	the ear
	light receptor cells	the eye
Effector	muscle cells	muscles
	hormone secreting cells	glands

Q4
1. Temperature receptors in Jamie's hand detect the increase in temperature.
2. Impulses travel along a sensory neurone.
3. The information is processed by the spinal cord.
4. Impulses travel along a motor neurone.
5. Some of the muscles in Jamie's hand contract, causing him to drop the pan.

Q5 Stimulus → Receptor → Sensory neurone → CNS → Motor Neurone → Effector → Response

Q6 a) As electrical impulses.
b) axon, cytoplasm, membrane
c) i) fatty sheath
ii) To increase the speed of transmission of a nerve impulse. To insulate the neurone from neighbouring cells.
d) i) synapse
ii) E.g. drugs, toxins.

Pages 73-74 — Reflexes

Q1 a) quickly
b) spinal cord, an unconscious
c) involuntary
d) protect
e) arc

Q2 a) stimulus, receptors, sensory, CNS, relay, motor, effector
b) i) Y
ii) Z
iii) X

Q3 They have difficulty responding to new situations.

Q4 a bird making its feathers stand on end — finding a mate
a turtle retracting its head and limbs into its shell — sheltering from a predator
a jellyfish moving its tentacles when it senses movement — finding food
a spider running onto its web when it feels it move — finding food
a mollusc closing its shell — sheltering from a predator

Q5 a) Eye A. The pupil has become smaller in this diagram to stop too much light entering the eye and damaging it.
b) reflex, quickly, adjust, damaged

Pages 75-76 — Brain Development and Learning

Q1 a) False
b) True
c) True

Q2 formed, developed, experience, more, stimulated, unconnected, network, trillions

Q3 Complex organisms have a larger variety of potential pathways in their brains.

Q4 repeated, pathways, strengthened, transmit

Q5 a) i) the cerebral cortex
ii) [Diagram of brain with Front, Back and Cerebral cortex labelled]
b) Any two of, e.g. intelligence / consciousness / language / memory.

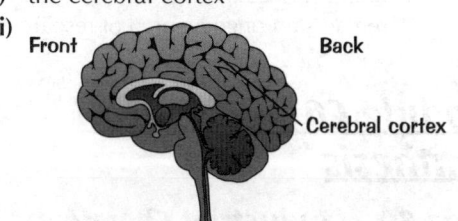

Page 77 — Studying the Brain

Q1 a) If a part of the brain has been damaged the effect this has on the patient can tell you a lot about what the damaged part of the brain does.

Module C6 — Chemical Synthesis

- **b)** By observing the effects of stimulating different parts of the brain, it's possible to get an idea what those parts do.
- **c)** MRI scans can be used to find out which areas of the brain are active when people are doing tasks like listening to music or trying to recall a memory.

Q2 a) short-term memory — includes things you're currently thinking about, lasts from a few seconds to a few hours
long-term memory — stored memories from days, weeks, months or years ago

b) The rides you went on when you visited a theme park last month. — L
The smell of hot apple pie drifting through from the kitchen as it's being baked. — S
What you had for tea last Wednesday. — L
Something that happened in an episode of The Bill half an hour ago. — S
What your great aunt Gladys got you for your birthday when you were fourteen. — L
Answering a question in an exam about a topic you learnt two months ago. — S

c) No model has yet been produced that provides an adequate explanation of memory.

Pages 78-79 — Memory Mapping

Q1 a) storage, retrieval
b) Studying patients with brain damage. / Electrically stimulating the brain. / MRI scans.
c) Long-term memory
d) temporal lobe
e) i) The ability to recall long-term memories. Short-term memories.
ii) The ability to form new long-term memories.
f) 'It is hoped that in the future a model will be devised that fully explains how our brains process memories — until then it remains an ongoing area of research.'

Module C6 — Chemical Synthesis

Page 80 — Industrial Chemical Synthesis

Q1 complex, simpler
Q2 a) small scale
b) large scale
Q3 a) Fertiliser production
b) 100 − 32 − 17 − 16 − 11 − 9 = **15%**
Q4 a) pharmaceuticals
b) 60 000

Pages 81-82 — Acids and Alkalis

Q1 a) neutral
b) 7
c) dyes/indicators/chemicals
d) greater

Q2 a) distilled water — pale green — 7 — neutral
b) rainwater — yellow — 5/6 — weak acid
c) caustic soda — purple — 14 — strong alkali
d) washing-up liquid — dark green/blue — 8/9 — weak alkali
e) car battery acid — red — 1 — strong acid

Q3 a) less, tartaric, solids, liquid, ethanoic/nitric, nitric/ethanoic, hydrogen chloride
b) E.g. sodium hydroxide, potassium hydroxide, calcium hydroxide.

Q4 a) acid + alkali → salt + water
b) i) aqueous hydrogen ions, $H^+(aq)$
ii) aqueous hydroxide ions, $OH^-(aq)$
c) i) [graph of pH vs Number of tablets: points at (0,1), (1,2), (2,3), (3,7), (4,7)]
ii) 3
d) E.g. using an indicator such as universal indicator / using a pH meter.

Q5 a) The hydrogen ions from the acid react with the hydroxide ions from the alkali to make water.
b) $H^+ + OH^- \rightarrow H_2O$

Page 83 — Acids Reacting with Metals

Q1 a) E.g. bubbles would be released and the metal would gradually disappear.
b) ACID + METAL → **salt** + **hydrogen**

Q2 a) False
b) True
c) False
d) False
e) True

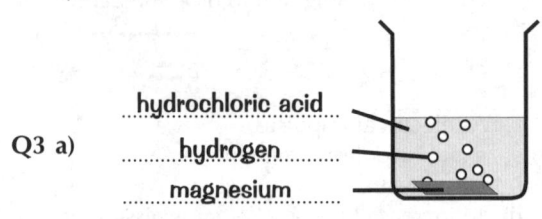

Q3 a) [diagram labelled: hydrochloric acid, hydrogen, magnesium]
b) magnesium + **hydrochloric acid** → magnesium chloride + **hydrogen**
c) zinc + sulfuric acid → zinc sulfate + hydrogen

Module C6 — Chemical Synthesis

Pages 84-85 — Oxides, Hydroxides and Carbonates

Q1 a) ACID + METAL OXIDE → **salt** + **water**
b) Copper oxide and hydrochloric acid.

Q2 a) ACID + METAL HYDROXIDE → **salt** + **water**
b) i) H_2SO_4(**aq**) + 2NaOH(**aq**) → Na_2SO_4(**aq**) + $2H_2O$(**l**)
ii) sulfuric acid + sodium hydroxide → sodium sulfate + water

Q3 a) hydrochloric acid + lead oxide → **lead** chloride + water.
b) nitric acid + copper hydroxide → copper **nitrate** + water.
c) sulfuric acid + zinc oxide → zinc sulfate + **water**
d) hydrochloric acid + **nickel** oxide → nickel **chloride** + **water**
e) **nitric** acid + copper oxide → **copper** nitrate + **water**
f) sulfuric acid + **sodium** hydroxide → sodium **sulfate** + **water**

Q4 a) ACID + METAL CARBONATE → **salt** + **water** + **carbon dioxide**
b) i) copper sulphate + water + carbon dioxide
ii) magnesium nitrate + water + carbon dioxide
iii) lithium sulfate + water + carbon dioxide
iv) calcium chloride + water + carbon dioxide
v) sodium sulfate + water + carbon dioxide
c) 2HCl(**aq**) + Na_2CO_3(**s**) → 2NaCl(**aq**) + H_2O(**l**) + CO_2(**g**)

Q5 a) i) Carbon dioxide gas is produced in the reaction.
ii) hydrochloric acid + copper carbonate → copper chloride + water + carbon dioxide
b) copper carbonate

Pages 86-88 — Synthesising Compounds

Q1 an acid and an alkali react to produce a salt — neutralisation
a compound breaks down on heating — thermal decomposition
an insoluble solid forms when two solutions are mixed — precipitation

Q2 a) injury, hazards, harmed, action, reduce
b) E.g. the amount of product and reactants / whether the reaction is explosive/gives out heat etc.

Q3 a) E.g. to isolate an insoluble product from the reaction mixture / to remove solid impurities from the liquid product.
b) To isolate a product that is dissolved in the reaction mixture/solvent.
c) To remove any water from the product.

Q4 a) neutralisation
b) Any two of, e.g. sodium hydroxide is highly reactive / sodium hydroxide is corrosive / a large amount of heat is produced in the reaction.
c) soluble / evaporated
d) E.g. crystallisation
e) i) a risk assessment
ii) E.g. it is harmful if swallowed and it can cause irritation to the skin and eyes.
f) The yield is calculated to give an indication of the overall success of the process.
g) i) pesticide production
ii) 100 − 42 − 22 − 15 − 11 − 4 = **6%**
iii) (11 ÷ 100) × 3000 = **330 tonnes**

Page 89 — Relative Formula Mass

Q1 a) mass, atom, carbon-12
b) i) 24
ii) 20
iii) 16
iv) 1
v) 12
vi) 63.5
vii) 39
viii) 40
ix) 35.5

Q2 Element A is helium
Element B's A_r is (3 × 4) = 12, so it is carbon
Element C's A_r is (4 × 4) = 16, so it is oxygen

Q3 a) You add the relative atomic masses of all the atoms in the compound together.
b) i) (2 × 1) + 16 = **18**
ii) 39 + 16 + 1 = **56**
iii) 1 + 14 + (3 × 16) = **63**
iv) 24 + ((16 + 1) × 2) = **58**
v) 56 + ((16 + 1) × 3) = **107**

Page 90 — Isolating the Product and Measuring Yield

Q1 a)
- This is the mass of pure dry product. It is found by **weighing** the dried product.
- percentage yield = (actual yield / theoretical yield) × 100
- This is the **actual yield** of the product as a percentage of the **theoretical yield**.
- This is the **maximum** amount of **pure**, dried product that could have been made using the amounts of **reactants** you started with.

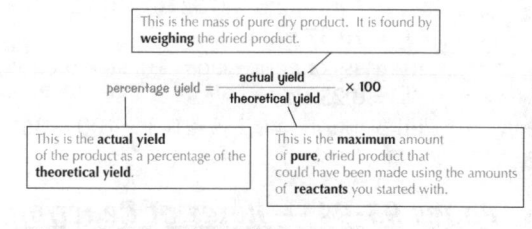

b) (1.2 ÷ 2.7) × 100 = **44.4%**
c) filtration
d) E.g. using a drying oven, using a desiccator.

Q2 a) evaporation and crystallisation
b) The crystals formed when a solution is evaporated have a regular structure which the impurities can't fit into.

Module C6 — Chemical Synthesis

Page 91 — Titrations

Q1 a) Titrations can't be carried out using solids, only liquids.

b)
- Crush the solid product into a powder.
- Weigh some of the powdered product into a titration flask.
- The powder is then dissolved by adding some solvent (e.g. water)
- Swirl the flask until all of the solid has dissolved.

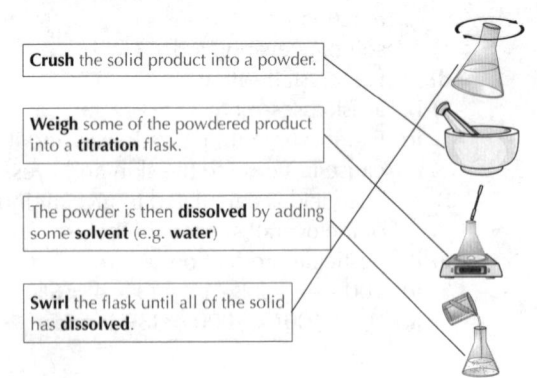

c) burette / titration/conical flask

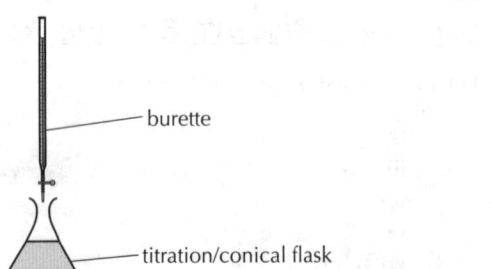

d) Add some alkali to a titration flask with a few drops of indicator. Fill a burette with acid. Add some acid to the alkali from the burette, regularly swirling the flask. Record the volume of acid when the indicator changes colour. (Titrations can also be carried out by adding alkali to acid.)

Page 92 — Purity

Q1 a) Any two of, e.g. filtration / evaporation / recrystallisation.
b) safe, dangerous

Q2 a) neutralisation
b) i) First calculate vol. of NaOH:
$21.6 \div 1000 = 0.0216$ dm³
Then the vol. of citric acid:
$25 \div 1000 = 0.025$ dm³
Concentration of citric acid
$= 4.8 \times [(2.5 \times 0.0216) \div 0.025]$
$= \mathbf{10.37}$ **g/dm³**
ii) Mass of citric acid = 10.37×0.025
= **0.259 g**
iii) % purity = $0.259 \div 0.3 \times 100$ = **86%**

Pages 93-94 — Rates of Reaction

Q1 a) Slow: an apple rotting; a ship rusting
Moderate speed: hair being dyed
Fast: a firework exploding; a match burning
b) reactants, products

Q2 safety, fast, explosion, economic, optimum, compromise, yield, costs

Q3 a) Q
b) R
c) [graph: Volume of gas produced vs Time (s), curves R, Q, P with X marked on R]

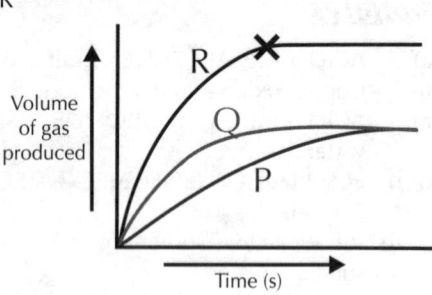

Q4 a) higher
b) lower
c) increases
d) increases

Q5 a) the volume of acid used / the temperature the reaction is carried out at / the size of the magnesium strips used
b) [graph: time (s) vs concentration (g/dm³)]
c) The more concentrated the acid, the faster the rate of the reaction.
d) increase

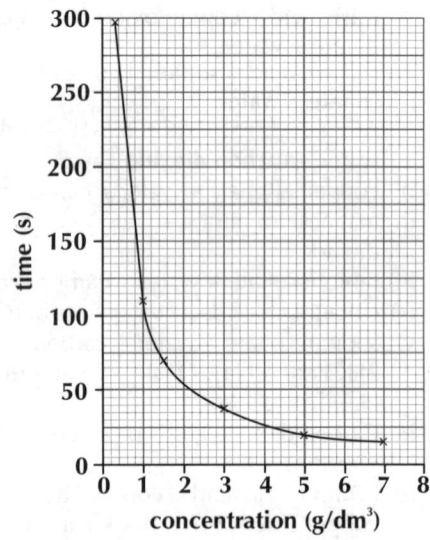

Page 95 — Measuring Rates of Reaction

Q1 speed, reactants, products

Q2 a) E.g. gas syringe / hydrochloric acid / magnesium
b) Place a flask containing the hydrochloric acid and magnesium onto a balance and record the change in mass over time.

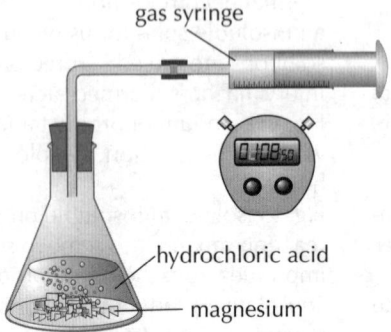

Module P6 — The Wave Model of Radiation

Q3 a) precipitation
b) Place the solution on a piece of paper with a mark drawn on it. Observe how long it takes for the mark to disappear.

Module P6 — The Wave Model of Radiation

Page 96 — Waves — The Basics

Q1 energy, matter
Q2 a) metres
b) There are 25 waves per second (emitted / passing a given point).
c) A
Q3 a) Transverse — 2, Longitudinal — 1.
b) E.g. transverse waves can travel in a vacuum but longitudinal waves cannot / vibrations in a transverse wave are perpendicular to the direction of travel, whereas in longitudinal waves they are parallel to the direction of travel.
Q4 a) He's drawn a wavelength of 4 m.
b) E.g.

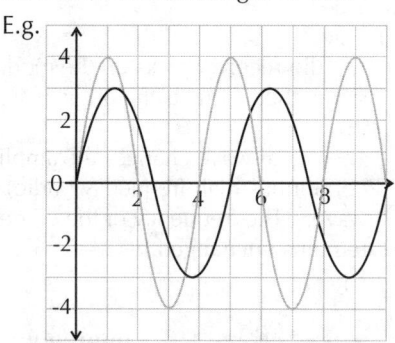

Q5 a) Ten waves every second = **10 Hz**
b) Speed = frequency × wavelength
   = 10 × 0.016
   = **0.16 m/s**

Page 97-99 — Wave Properties

Q1 a) A line at right angles to the surface.
b)

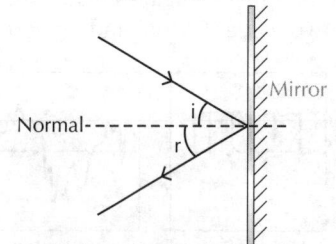

Q2 a) When a wave slows down, the wavelength **gets shorter**. The frequency **stays the same**. The wave may bend **towards** the normal.
b) When a wave speeds up, the wavelength **gets longer**. The frequency **stays the same**. The wave may bend **away from** the normal.
Q3 a) air, glass, faster, towards
b) away from

Q4 a) B
b) Because the waves are meeting the boundary at right angles.
c) i) The wavelength gets shorter.
   ii) The frequency remains the same.
   iii) The waves slow down.
d)

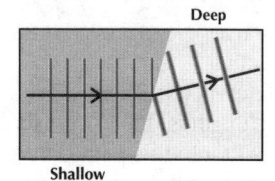

(The wave would speed up again — the wavelength would increase and the frequency would stay the same.)
Q5 a) completely, boundary, dense, less dense
b) B
Q6 incidence, denser, internally
Q7

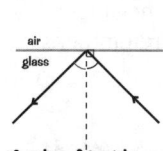

Angle of incidence greater than 42°   Angle of incidence less than 42°   Angle of incidence is 42°

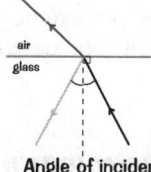

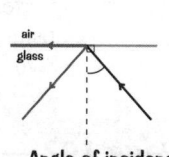

Q8 a) Diffraction is the spreading out of a wave when it travels through a gap or past an object.
b)

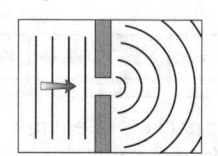

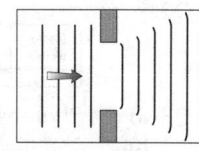

c) A window is much wider/taller than the wavelength of light.

Pages 100-101 — Wave Interference

Q1 a)

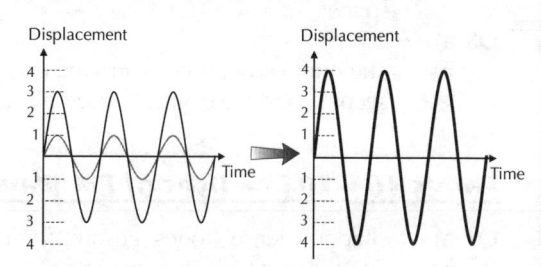

This is **constructive** interference.
b)

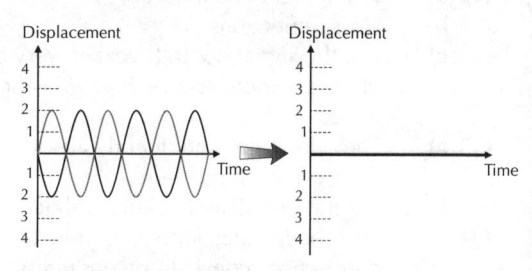

This is **destructive** interference.

Module P6 — The Wave Model of Radiation

Q2 a) constructive interference
   b) The difference in the distance travelled by two waves.
   c) B
   d) The distance would increase.
Q3 a) A — constructive
       B — constructive
       C — destructive
       D — destructive
   b) i) The path difference is **3 cm**.
      ii) Half a wavelength is 0.5 cm, so **six** half-wavelengths fit into this path difference.
      iii) Six is an even number, so there will be **constructive** interference.
   c) i) The path difference is still **3 cm**.
      ii) Half a wavelength is now 1 cm, so **three** half-wavelengths fit into this path difference.
      iii) Three is an odd number, so there will be **destructive** interference.
Q4 interference, positive/negative, negative/positive, light/dark, dark/light, reinforce, wave

Page 102 — Electromagnetic Radiation

Q1 a) False
   b) False
   c) False
   d) True
Q2

Radio waves	Micro-waves	Infrared	VISIBLE LIGHT	Ultraviolet	X-rays	Gamma rays

Q3 a) Photons are tiny packets of energy.
   b) The higher the **frequency** of the radiation, the **greater** the amount of energy carried by each photon.
Q4 Sound waves are longitudinal, so they're carried by vibrating particles and therefore can't travel through a vacuum such as space.
Q5 a) C
   b) The number of photons arriving each second, and the energy carried by each.

Pages 103-104 — Uses of EM Waves

Q1 a) shadow, dense, bones, absorb, flesh, less
   b) E.g. scanning luggage in airports.
Q2 a) visible light and infrared
   b) glass, reflections
   c) E.g. the signal doesn't weaken very quickly / they are more secure than wires or radio waves.
Q3 a) They don't get significantly absorbed by the Earth's atmosphere.
   b) E.g. TV broadcasts / walkie talkies
Q4 absorbed, water, kinetic, conduction/convection, convection/conduction

Q5 a) 1. Gabrielle's phone sends a microwave signal to...
       2. ...a communications satellite...
       3. ...orbiting above the Earth's atmosphere.
       4. The satellite absorbs the signal and then retransmits it to...
       5. ...a ground station...
       6. ...near Toronto, which sends the signal to...
       7. ...Carwyn's phone.
   b) Metal reflects microwaves well, so that the waves can be focused onto the receiver rather than absorbed by the dish.
   c) Certain frequencies of microwave can travel easily through the atmosphere.

Page 105 — Adding Information to Waves

Q1 signals, telephone lines, EM waves, visible light/infrared, infrared/visible light
Q2 a) frequency modulation
   b) i) True
      ii) False
      iii) True
      iv) True
   c) A radio receiver picks up the modulated wave, then extracts the original signal from it.
Q3 a) The signal wave changes the amplitude of a continuous high-frequency (radio) carrier wave. (The frequency of the carrier wave remains unchanged.)
   b) E.g.

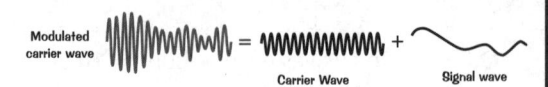

Modulated carrier wave = Carrier Wave + Signal wave

Page 106 — Analogue and Digital Signals

Q1 a) Analogue signals can take any value within a certain range. Digital signals can only take two values — 'on' and 'off' / 0 or 1.
   b) E.g.

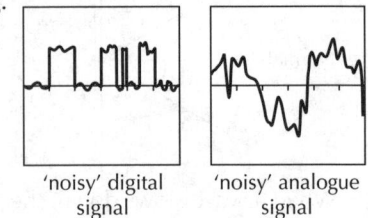

'noisy' digital signal   'noisy' analogue signal

Q2 weaken, intensity, amplified, interference, analogue

Module P6 — The Wave Model of Radiation

Q3 E.g. Computers process digital information only (analogue signals would have to be converted from and to digital ones) / more information can be sent using a digital signal than an analogue signal at one time / digital signals are easier to encrypt. (Other answers are possible.)

Pages 107-108 — Broadband and Wireless Internet

Q1 a) E.g. broadband connections are faster than dial-up connections, so are better at downloading large music and video files.

b) i) $(14\,000\,000 \div 25\,000\,000) \times 100\%$
= **56%**

ii) 75% of households with access to the internet have a broadband connection.
$0.75 \times 14\,000\,000 = 10\,500\,000$
= **10.5 million**.

c) i) layer B
ii) layer A

d) i) transverse
ii) speed = frequency × wavelength
= $2\,400\,000\,000 \times 0.125$
= **300 000 000 m/s**
iii) digital

e) E.g. the range of a wireless router is about 100 m, so surrounding houses can probably intercept your router's radio signal. They could therefore potentially interfere with your computers / 'steal' your internet connection.

ISBN 978 1 84762 005 7

S1FA41